Task Listening
Teacher's Book

Task Listening

Teacher's Book

Lesley Blundell and Jackie Stokes

CAMBRIDGE
UNIVERSITY PRESS

Published by the Press Syndicate of the University of Cambridge
The Pitt Building, Trumpington Street, Cambridge CB2 1RP
40 West 20th Street, New York, NY 10011–4211, USA
10 Stamford Road, Oakleigh, Melbourne 3166, Australia

© Cambridge University Press 1991

First published 1981
Fifteenth printing 1996

Printed in Great Britain by
J. W. Arrowsmith Ltd, Bristol

ISBN 0 521 23136 1 Teacher's Book
ISBN 0 521 23135 3 Student's Book
ISBN 0 521 23137 X Cassette

Publisher's note
For details of sources of illustrations and other copyright material
please see the Student's book.

Contents

Introduction

Task Listening aims to provide flexible listening materials for students who have had little exposure to unscripted spoken English. They might be post-elementary students studying in Britain, more advanced students whose listening has been developed primarily as a means to a structural or grammatical end, or anyone who wants to brush up their English.

Task Listening helps students overcome their difficulties in understanding English spoken at normal speed by using short, unscripted recordings of people speaking in a number of everyday situations. When listening to authentic speech students often find it difficult to recognise the items of language they had previously learnt. With this material, the teacher prepares students for listening by presenting or revising the key language for each recording so that they know what to listen for. Another difficulty can be speed. This arises because the student tends to try to catch every word and often comprehends little as a result. *Task Listening* aims to help students understand the overall message rather than listen for every detail.

There are twenty-six units. Each has as its theme a setting or situation in which listening plays a major part, for example, at an airport listening for flight announcements, or at a travel agency being told about different means of transport. Each unit consists of a tape recording and a related listening task; thematically linked reading and writing tasks are provided as a follow-up to each listening task. Instead of comprehension questions there are listening tasks which take the form of practical exercises, such as labelling diagrams, filling in missing information and compiling lists. The nature of these tasks varies to give the student practice in a number of listening activities: gist listening, sifting and labelling, note-taking, deducing. The units have been ordered according to the length of the recording, the number and speed of the speakers and the type of task. Bearing this in mind the teacher is free to use the units in any order.

The Teacher's Book

Extensive notes are provided on each unit beginning with a tapescript and details about the tape, i.e. length, number of speakers and setting.

There are lists of key functions, lexis and structures for each recording and suggestions for the preparation and revision of this key language. Structural items such as phrasal verbs are often listed under 'Lexis' to indicate that they should be taught as one-off vocabulary items. Only the items listed under 'Structures' need be presented and practised so that students can use them with relative ease in their own production of language.

Notes are provided on each listening task. Students can listen to the recording as many times as necessary, secure in knowing they are familiar with the language vital to the successful completion of the task. You should refrain from asking comprehension questions between each playing of the recording since this detracts from the function of the listening task. *Task Listening* aims to help train students to sift out those utterances of relevance and to ignore redundant features, a skill vital to efficient listening at all levels of language learning.

Notes are provided on each reading and writing task.

Completed task pages appear at the end of each unit. The answers given are only examples of possible correct answers in some cases.

1 Catching the right train

Objectives

1 To give students practice in listening to railway announcements made over the loudspeaker system and in sifting out the information relevant to specific journeys.
2 To give students practice in
   a) reading a railway timetable;
   b) picking out information relevant to a specific journey;
   c) writing a postcard re time of arrival.

Tape

Tapescript

The train now standing at platform 4 is the 11.04 to Bournemouth, calling at Reading, Basingstoke, Southampton and Bournemouth.

The next train to arrive at platform 5 will be the 11.05 to Birmingham New Street, calling at Banbury, Leamington Spa, Dorridge, Solihull, Coventry, Birmingham International and Birmingham New Street.

The 11.31 inter-city train to Exeter and Plymouth has been delayed. This train is now running approximately fifteen minutes late and is now due to arrive at platform 1 at 11.46. We apologise to passengers for the delay.

The train now arriving at platform 2 is the 11.10 to Paddington London, calling at Didcot and Reading.

We are sorry to announce that the 11.20 train to Cardiff Central has been cancelled due to a derailment. Passengers for Cardiff should take the 11.10 London train and change at Didcot.

The inter-city train to Newcastle will arrive at platform 6 at 11.40. Passengers for York and Newcastle should change at Birmingham New Street.

Length: 1 min. 40 sec.
Number of speakers: 1.
Setting: Train information being relayed over a loudspeaker system at a station.

Key language

Function: Giving information about the running times of trains.

Lexis:
train	change at
platform	due to arrive
inter-city	running late
the next train	delay
the 11.20 train	cancel
passengers for	take the train
calling at	

Structures: The train now arriving at ...
The train now standing at ...
The next train to arrive will be ...
The train will arrive at ...
The train has been delayed
The train has been cancelled

TEACHING HINTS

Most students will have travelled by train and will be able to tell you the kind of information heard over the loudspeaker system. You will probably find that you can feed in a lot of the key lexis here as required.

To follow the tape and be able to complete the task, students need only a passive understanding of the structures. The most important thing for students to understand is whether the train is in the station at the time of speaking or will arrive in the future.

This unit could usefully follow some earlier dialogue work on getting train information. It could also be used as an extension to situational dialogue work 'At the station'.

Tasks

Before listening

Ask students to look at the tickets on page 2 in their books. Students who know England well will be able to tell the others where the towns and cities on the tickets can be found. Alternatively use a map of England to locate these places. Tell them they are going to hear some announcements made at a station.

Listening task

Tell students that their task is to fill in details of the trains on the grid. Explain that it is not necessary to write the platform number and time in long hand. Ask students to predict the kinds of information they will have to write under 'Other information' and point out that only brief details are needed. Let them check their answers with each other then with you.

Reading task

Ask students to read the letter and underline those parts which they do not understand. Encourage them to help each other and to deduce the meaning from the context. Good dictionaries are obviously helpful but students should try to see the function of sentences such as 'Why don't you get a train from Paddington...' A word-for-word translation would provide a totally inappropriate explanation. If the railway timetable extract differs greatly from those with which the students are familiar, you may have to explain how to read the timetable. Some explanation of the twenty-four-hour clock and its pronunciation may also be necessary. Now ask the students to choose a convenient train for Peter to catch after work on Friday.

Writing task

When the reading task has been completed students simply enter the train details on the postcard. The rest of the postcard can be completed by referring to the beginning and end of the letter.

1 Catching the right train

Listening

Fill in the details of the trains on the grid.

Destination	Platform Number	Time	Other Information
SOUTHAMPTON	4	11.04	
COVENTRY	5	11.05	
PLYMOUTH	1	11.46	15 minutes late
PADDINGTON	2	11.10	
CARDIFF	2	11.10	Change at Didcot CARDIFF TRAIN DERAILED
YORK	6	11.40	Change at Birmingham New Street

Completed writing task

32 Abercrombie Ave,
Coventry,
Sunday evening.

Dear Peter,

Thank you for your postcard from Italy. We were pleased to hear you enjoyed yourself.

Yes we'd love you to come on the 27th for the weekend. Why don't you get a train from Paddington after work on Friday? Write to us and say when you'll arrive at Coventry and we'll meet you at the station.

See you on Friday
Love from
Andrew and Jenny

Choose a suitable train for Peter to catch and complete his postcard to Andrew and Jenny.

London → Reading → Oxford → Banbury → Birmingham **Mondays to Saturdays**											Birmingham New Street
Paddington	Reading	Didcot	Oxford	Banbury	Leamington Spa	Stratford-upon-Avon	Dorridge	Solihull	Coventry	Birmingham International	
							arrivals	17 58			18 18
								18 21	18 28	18 41	18 40
						18 16	18 32				18 58
departures			16 51	17 18	17 37						
	16 30		17 15	17 42	18 02						20 06
15 50	16 20		17 36								20 58
	16 41	17 03	17 45	18 17				17 58		20 41	21 40
	17 04	17 03	18 36	18 58				19 48	20 28	21 27	
16 25	17 04			19 07	19 27	20 16	19 42	21 08	21 04		23 21
16 25	18 00	18 20			20 14	21 31	21 02	22 02			
17 30			19 29	20 31	20 50		21 56				
17 42	18 57	18 46	20 05	20 50				22 58			
18 06	19 30	19 48	20 20	22 21	22 41	23 17					
19 00			21 55								
20 50	21 20	21 38									

RIBMINGHAM
INTERNATIONAL
7 OCT
1980
C

Dear Andrew & Jenny,
Thank you **for your letter**
I'm going to get the **6.06 train** from Paddington. So
I will arrive at **8.28 on Friday.**
I hope you'll be able to meet me.
See **you on Friday,**
Love from Peter.

Be properly addressed
POSTCODE IT

Andrew & Jenny Brown
32 Abercrombie Ave.
Coventry

PLX14128

2 Catching a plane

Objectives

1 To give students practice in understanding airport announcements.
2 To give students practice in reading official airport information and sifting out the information relevant to their needs.

Tape

Tapescript

British Airways announce the departure of Flight 720 to Paris. Boarding now at Gate 7.

This is the final call for British Airways Flight 504 to Brussels. Boarding now at Gate 21.

This is an urgent call for passenger Mr Richard Chisholm. Would Mr Chisholm please go to the Airport Information Desk.

British Caledonian announce the departure of Flight 107 to Ibiza. Boarding now at Gate 17.

This is the final call for Alitalia Flight 409 to Milan. Boarding now at Gate 3.

British Airways regret that all flights are subject to delay. This is due to a shortage of baggage handlers.

British Airways announce the departure of Flight 191 to Madrid. Boarding now at Gate 11.

Length: 1 min. 25 sec.
Number of speakers: 1.
Setting: Announcements being relayed over the loudspeaker system in an airport departure lounge.

Key language

Function: Giving information and instructions to passengers.

Lexis:		
announce	final call	
departure	urgent	
flight	regret	
boarding at	subject to delay	
gate		

Structures: BA announce...
Would... please go to...
This is the...

The structures listed are not crucial to an understanding of the tape, but may be taught or revised in conjunction with the listening task. Teach the lexis in the context of air travel. Find a picture or wall chart to use as a visual aid.

Tasks

Before listening

Find out which students have travelled by air. Ask them if they liked it, if it was easy to do, what they liked best/least etc. Check that they know that the other name for London Airport is Heathrow Airport and that the largest airline is called British Airways. Then ask them if it is easy to understand official announcements at airports and railways. Tell them to open their books at page 4 and tell you what the picture is showing. Tell them they are going to hear some announcements made at an airport.

Listening task

Tell students that their task is to fill in the missing information in the spaces provided in the bubbles. Let them check their answers with each other and then with you.

Reading and writing tasks

First ask students if it is easy to read air or train timetables. If they say no, contradict them and tell them to open their books at page 5. Give them a minute to look at the London–Frankfurt timetable and then guide them through it by asking focus questions, for example, 'Does the 14.10 plane fly on Tuesdays?' 'Do you go to Terminal 2 for the 10.05 flight?' 'Can you travel first class on the 16.45 flight?' etc. When they can read that satisfactorily, present the task and then ask them to complete everything they can for Mr Browning. Check their answers with them. Then ask them to look at the Airport Information chart and help them by asking focus questions such as 'Will £1 be enough to pay for an airport bus ticket from London to Heathrow?' 'What do I do at Heathrow if I want Terminal 2?' 'My flight is at 11.25 and I must go to Terminal 1. It is now 10 a.m. Am I late?' When they can read this chart satisfactorily, ask them to complete some more notes for Mr Browning. Check their answers. For the last note, ask students to look at the list of telephone numbers for enquiries and fill in the right one. Now ask them if they feel better about reading airport information in English.

2 Catching a plane

Listening

Fill in the missing information.

Reading and writing

Mr Browning must be at his hotel in Frankfurt at 3.00 p.m. (15.00) for a meeting. It takes 30 minutes to get to his hotel from Frankfurt Airport. Complete the notes at the bottom of the page for him.

LONDON—FRANKFURT   British airways / Associate Hotels

DEPART London, Heathrow Airport. BA flights: Terminal 1 (Minimum check-in time at pier gate 20 mins) Other flights: Terminal 2 (Minimum check-in time 30 mins) London, Gatwick Airport [G] (Minimum check-in time 30 mins)
ARRIVE Frankfurt-on-Main Airport

Frequency	Aircraft Dep	Arr	Via	Flight	Aircraft	Class & Catering	
Daily	0820	1045(y)	non-stop	BA724	TRD	FY	✗
Daily	1005	1230	non-stop	LH033	AB3	FY	✗
Daily	1105	1230	non-stop	LH033	AB3	FY	✗
Daily	1125	1350(y)	non-stop	BA726	TRD	FY	✗
Daily	1410	1635	non-stop	LH035	727	FY	✗
Daily	1455	1625	non-stop	LH035	727	FY	✗
Daily	1605 [G]	1825(y)	non-stop	BA784	B11	Y	❢❢
Daily	1645	1910(y)	non-stop	BA728	L10 (a)	FY	✗
Daily	1750	1915	non-stop	BA730	TRD	FY	✗
Daily	1810	2035	non-stop	LH037	AB3	FY	✗
Daily	1850	2115	non-stop	BA730	TRD	FY	✗
Daily	1910	2035	non-stop	LH037	AB3	FY	✗

Class of service
F First class
Y Economy

Catering
✗ Meal — i.e. full breakfast, lunch, dinner or supper
❢❢ Flight snack/Continental breakfast/Refreshment/Afternoon tea

AIRPORT INFORMATION

Place	Transport to Airport Address and coach departure time (in minutes) before aircraft departure and other Surface Connections	Single Fare	Airport Minimum check-in time in mins.
BRITISH ISLES (cont.)			
London (LON)	Coaches depart Victoria Terminal at frequent intervals throughout the day for Terminals 1 and 3. Passengers for Terminal 2 alight at Terminals 1 and walk across connecting bridge. Telephone 01 821 4074/4075 for coach services. Passengers are advised to join a coach not later than: Terminal 1 (International flights)— 120 minutes before scheduled departure time of aircraft (165 minutes for flights to Tel Aviv). Terminal 1 (Inter-Britain flights)— 110 minutes before scheduled departure time of aircraft. Terminal 3 Coaches from Victoria Terminal: Minimum check-in time 2 hours 15 minutes before aircraft departure time. Terminal 2 Check-in times vary according to carrier and should be verified prior to departure.	£1.70 £1.70	See relevant schedule table
London (Gatwick)	Gatwick Airport. Frequent trains from Victoria Station.	£3.15 (1st) £2.10 (2nd)	BA, EI, GT, SK·30Int.

FLIGHT ARRIVAL/DEPARTURE ENQUIRIES AT PRINCIPAL UK AIRPORTS

To obtain information concerning flight arrivals and departures, on the day of travel, at the following airports, telephone:—

Aberdeen	72-2331	Edinburgh	031-333 1000	London (Heathrow)	01-759 2525
Belfast	29271	Glasgow	041-887 1111	,, (Gatwick)	Crawley (0293) 502064
Birmingham	021-743 4272	Prestwick	0292 79822	Manchester	061-437 5277
Inverness	Ardersier 2280	Newcastle	Newcastle 869081		

Depart from ....**Heathrow**.... Airport at ....**11.25**.... a.m.

Get to Airport from ....**Victoria Terminal**....

Transport costs £....**1.70**....

Leave ....**120**.... minutes before departure time of aircraft.

Be at Transport Terminal by ....**9.25**.... a.m.

Flight number ....**BA 726**....   Type of aircraft ....**TRD**....

Food during flight ....**Yes- lunch**....   Arrival time ....**13.50**.... p.m.

If the weather is bad on day of flight, ring ....**01-759 2525**....

for flight details.

9

3　Forecasting the weather

Objectives

1　To help students to understand and follow a weather forecast.
2　To give students the chance to read a humorous account of the kind of comments the English make about the weather.

Tape

Tapescript

Newscaster:　...and that's the end of the news. Now we'll go over to the weather centre for the weather forecast for the whole of the United Kingdom.

Weatherman:　Good evening. Due to the depression lying off the north of England and the high in the south of England, tomorrow's weather will be variable across the country. Starting, then, in the south-west, it'll start cool and become warm with long periods of sunshine. Around London and the south-east, the day will be dry but cloudy at times. In the Midlands, it'll be cloudy all day with showers at times. Moving over, then, to North Wales, there may be fog patches over the mountains for probably much of the day, while in South Wales it'll be generally windy. In the north-east, it'll be cloudy all day, some rain everywhere and it'll be heavy at times. Further north in Scotland, we can expect sleet in those areas south of Edinburgh, while in the very north of Scotland and the Hebrides, there'll be snow on high ground. Now in Northern Ireland, there's a possibility of rain, and it'll certainly be very cold. That's the end of the weather forecast.

Length: 1 min. 9 sec.
Number of speakers: 2.
Setting: Weatherman reading the weather forecast.

Key language

Function: Describing what the weather will be.

Lexis:	
south-west	Midlands
south-east	Hebrides
north-east	North Wales
south of Edinburgh	Northern Ireland
very north of Scotland	around
further north	periods

sunshine	rain
cold	heavy
warm	windy
dry	snow
cloudy	sleet
showers	fog

Structures: The day will be...

... becoming...

There's a possibility of...

TEACHING HINTS

The descriptions of the weather, e.g. 'cloudy with showers', can best be taught by asking students to look at the key on page 6. Many of these terms can be guessed by looking at the symbols.

Use the map of Britain to teach the remaining lexis. The structures need little more than a brief mention. Point out that the structure 'The day will be...' is one that weathermen use when forecasting the weather and that any other person would probably say 'It's going to ...'

Tasks

Before listening

Ask any students who have been to Britain to show the others, on the map, where they stayed. Some students may know the cities and towns marked on the map, ask them to tell you what they can about the places.

Listening task

Tell students to choose one of the places marked on the map. Now, tell them they are going to hear a weather forecast and they should listen for the forecast for the city they have chosen. Play the tape until everyone has done this. Ask them to look at the key around the map and find the symbol which depicts the weather forecast for their chosen city and to draw this on the map. This can be repeated as many times as you feel it would be useful. Let them check their answers with each other and with you.

Reading task

Any of your students who has been to England will be able to tell you two things about English weather. Firstly, that it always rains and secondly that Englishmen continually talk about it. The reading for this unit is from *How to be an Alien* by George Mikes, the passage is meant to equip the foreigner with useful phrases for conversing about the weather.

Ask students to read the extract and to guess the meanings of those phrases they have not come across before. This passage should be dealt with lightly and enjoyed, so do not dwell on the differences between the phrases. It is certainly worth reading these phrases aloud with the class as the stress and intonation is so important to the meaning.

11

Writing task

Ask students to look at the three cartoons and to suggest what the characters are saying about the weather. When they have decided on a comment for each cartoon, either one from the list or one they have thought up themselves, ask them to write it down. When everyone has finished go round and see if there are any particularly funny ones and show these to the rest of the class, otherwise ask everyone to pass their books round.

3 Forecasting the weather

Listening

Choose one of the places on the map and listen for the weather forecast for that area. Draw the correct symbol on the map.

with long periods of sunshine

cool becoming warmer

cold

dry

cloudy with showers at times

cloudy with some rain, heavy at times

windy

snow

sleet

fog

INVERNESS

EDINBURGH

BELFAST

DUBLIN

BIRMINGHAM

CARDIFF

LONDON

N
W — E
S

Reading and writing

THE WEATHER

THIS is the most important topic in the land. Do not be misled by memories of your youth when, on the Continent, wanting to describe someone as exceptionally dull, you remarked: 'He is the type who would discuss the weather with you.' In England this is an ever-interesting, even thrilling topic, and you must be good at discussing the weather.

EXAMPLES FOR CONVERSATION

For Good Weather

'Lovely day, isn't it?'
'Isn't it *beautiful*?'
'The sun . . .'
'Isn't it gorgeous?'
'Wonderful, isn't it?'
'It's so nice and hot . . .'
'Personally, I think it's so nice when it's hot– isn't it?'
'I adore it – don't you?'

For Bad Weather

'Nasty day, isn't it?'
'Isn't it dreadful?'
'The rain . . . I hate rain . . .'
'I don't like it at all. Do you?'
'Fancy such a day in July. Rain in the morning, then a bit of sunshine, and then rain, rain, rain, all day long.'
'I remember exactly the same July day in 1936.'
'Yes, I remember too.'
'Or was it in 1928?'
'Yes, it was.'
'Or in 1939?'
'Yes, that's right.'

What do you think is being said in these cartoons? Write captions for each one.

'Nasty day, isn't it.'

'Fancy such a day in July!'

'The rain... I hate rain...'

14

4 Sightseeing

Objectives

1 To give students practice in sifting a tourist guide's patter to extract basic, specific information.
2 To give students practice in reading tourist maps and charts of information and in writing a personal postcard based on that information.

Tape

Tapescript

Tourist guide: We're travelling down Abbey Hill Road and on the left-hand side you can see the Palace of Holyrood House. Next-door to the palace you can see an abbey. This was built in 1128 by King David of Scotland and it was built as a penance because he went hunting on a Sunday which was not allowed in Scotland at this time. Now we're going to turn right down Canon Gate and High Street and Lawn Market. Now all these three roads together are called the Royal Mile which is the distance, supposedly, between the Palace of Holyrood House and Edinburgh Castle. On your right-hand side, just coming up, is the house of John Knox – a man who was a Calvinist preacher and he was the man who I'm going to talk about later on our journey when we reach St Giles's Church. The house he lived in is now a museum. And on the left is St Giles's Cathedral where John Knox actually preached. Now this was built in the fourteenth and fifteenth century and was renovated in the sixteenth century. Next to St Giles's Cathedral is the Heart of Midl... Midlothian. It's a heart-shaped design in the pavement. And this is where the old tolbooth prison gate was. We're now going up towards Edinburgh Castle, and this dates mainly from the eleventh century, where Queen Margaret's Chapel is. That's the oldest part of Edinburgh Castle and in fact the oldest building in Edinburgh. The rest of it was destroyed by Robert the Bruce. But now I think we can get out of the coach and have a look at Edinburgh Castle.

Length: 2 min. 10 sec.
Number of speakers: 1.
Setting: On board a tourist coach, travelling down the Royal Mile in Edinburgh with a guide giving information through a microphone.

Key language

Function: Identifying buildings and giving basic historical information.

Lexis: on the left-hand side   on the left
     on your right-hand side   preach
     palace   heart-shaped
     next-door to   pavement
     abbey   in the ...th century
     museum   oldest

Structures: you can see...
     this was built...
     ...are called...
     we're going to turn right
     down...
     the distance between ... and ...
     we're going up towards...

TEACHING HINTS

Present and practise any new lexis and structures in the context of a tour of a
town or city the students all know well. Either draw a map on the board or use a
large tourist map. Practise each item or pattern as it is presented and frequently
return to the start to practise again those items already taught. For further
practice, ask students in pairs to give each other tours of their own town or a very
well known city. The students acting as tourists should guess the town or city
being described.

Tasks

Before listening

Locate Edinburgh on a map of Scotland, show students some pictures of it if
possible, and interest them in the historical and archeological attractions of the
city. Find out what they think tourist guides talk about, whether they think
they're boring or interesting etc. Ask them to open their books at page 8 and
identify the town. Tell them they are going to hear a tourist guide on a coach
giving information to the passengers about Edinburgh.

Listening task

Tell students to listen in order to find the descriptions to go with the buildings
numbered on the map. Ask them to put the correct number beside each
description. Then tell them to listen again in order to fill in all the missing
information. Let them check their answers in pairs and then ask them to give you
the number of each place. Check the missing information by asking them to give
you all the information they know about each place.

    To round the session off, ask the students if they would like to go to Edinburgh,
which buildings they would choose to visit and whether they would like to be
tourist guides.

Reading task

Find out if anyone has been to Wales. Locate it on a map of the British Isles. Briefly describe the kinds of countryside you can find there – mountains, green valleys, moors, sheep, lakes, waterfalls, few houses except in the mining area to the south and the large towns or tourist centres. Tell students that there is a Welsh language, ask them to open their books at page 9 and to find any names that look strange (e.g. Llanelli). Next ask them to identify all the places of interest numbered on the map by looking at the chart of Major Attractions. Check comprehension of the chart by asking, for example, if the Snowdon Mountain Railway is open in winter or if the Trefriw Woollen Mills are open on Sundays. Then ask them to look at the chart at the bottom of the page and try to read it for one minute. Help them to do this by focussing their attention on specific items. Ask them, for example, the name of the inn in Trefriw, its telephone number, the minimum price of a double room, whether you can take a dog there etc. Finally ask them to choose a place to stay and three places of interest to visit. They can either do this individually or as a class.

Writing task

Having selected somewhere to stay and three places to visit, students should imagine the kind of things that happen on this holiday. Help them to do this by telling them how you got stuck in your car in a flock of sheep or how you got lost in the mountains! Then make a list on the board of such occurrences under the headings: accommodation, food, transport, people. When students have got into the situation, tell them they have bought a picture postcard of Rhuddlan Castle to send to an English friend. Draw a postcard on the board, write it with the whole class and then ask them to write their own for homework.

4 Sightseeing

Listening

Put the correct number in the box beside each description. Then fill in the missing information.

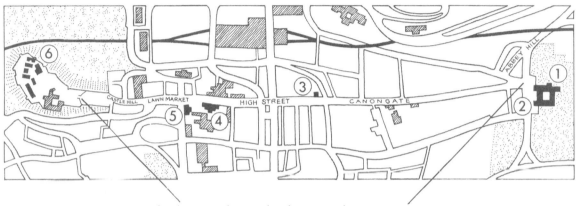

The three roads together between these two points are called .. **the Royal Mile** ....

THINGS TO SEE IN EDINBURGH

2 Abbey: built in ...**1128**.... by King David of Scotland.

5 Heart of Midlothian is a heart-shaped design in the ..**pavement**.....

6 Edinburgh Castle: part of this, Queen Margaret's chapel is the ...**oldest**..... building in Edinburgh.

3 John Knox House: now a ....**museum**...........

1 The Palace of Holyrood ...**House**.......

4 St Giles's Cathedral: where ...**John Knox**........... preached.

Reading and writing

North Wales' Major Attractions

SPRING ▭ ● Season open
SUMMER ▨ ○ Day open
AUTUMN ▨
WINTER ▨

		Monday	Tuesday	Wednesday	Thursday	Friday	Saturday	Sunday
1	Portmeirion	●	●	●		○	○	○	○
2	Rhuddlan Castle	●	●	●		○	○	○	○
3	Rhyl Floral Hall	●	●	●		○	○	○	○
4	St. Winifreds Well, Holywell	●	●	●	●	○	○	○	○
5	Segontium Roman Fort	●	●	●		○	○	○	○
6	Snowdon Mountain Railway, Llanberis	●	●	●		○	○	○	○
7	Sun Centre, Rhyl	●	●	●		○	○	○	○
8	Swallow Falls, Betws-y-Coed	●	●	●		○	○	○	○
9	Tegfryn Art Gallery, Menai Bridge	●	●	●	●	○	○	○	○
10	Trefriw Woollen Mills	●	●	●	●	○	○	○	○
11	Welsh Mountain Zoo, Colwyn Bay	●	●	●		○	○	○	○

Write a postcard to an English friend about your holiday in Wales.

COLOURMASTER
INTERNATIONAL
CA 58

Dear David,
   I'm having a lovely time. We're staying on a farm and the food is very good. Yesterday we went to see Segontium Roman fort. It was very interesting. Today we are at Rhuddlan's Castle. It's great.
   Best wishes,
   Juan

POST OFFICE
PREFERRED
Printed in
Great Britain

Mr D. Miles
11 King's Road
Campton
Kent

PLX14127

Hotels, Motels, Inns and Guest Houses

Town (County) Hotel Address Telephone number	Overnight bed and breakfast Min. / Max.	Dinner, bed and breakfast Min.	Full board Min. / Max.	Weekly terms Min. / Max.	Number of letting rooms	Private / Public bathrooms	Period open months	Other facilities
	£ £	£	£ £	£ £			1-12	
TREFRIW Gwynedd (Caernarvonshire)								
Inn								
Ye Olde Ship *T. Llanrwst 640013*		7·50			3		1 1-12	P ✕ C ⌂
Guest Houses								
Argoed *T. Llanrwst 640091*			32·00		2	1 1		P UL ☙ C
Gaynor House *T. Llanrwst 640208*	3·50	7·00	35·00		2 2 3	1 1-12	P UL ✕ C ⌂
Trefriw Wells *T. Llanrwst 640057*	5·50	10·00			1 4	1 1 1-12	P ✕ C ▤
Private Houses								
Belmont, Ffordd Crafnant								
T. Llanrwst 640463		7·00	35·00		2	1 4-10	P UL ✕ C ▤
Kendal *T. Llanrwst 640200*	3·25		35·00		2 1	1 1-12	P UL C ⌂
Tan-y-Coed *T. Llanrwst 640766*	3·50 4·00	6·00	35·00		4 1	1 1-12	P UL ✕ C ▤ ⌂

P Outdoor parking available.

UL Not licensed for sale of alcoholic drinks.

✕ Dogs not allowed under any circumstances. If this symbol does not appear it is still advisable to contact the establishment concerned.

☙ Childrens cots and high chairs and baby sitting/listening service available.

C Reduced Rates for children.

⌂ Ironing facilities available for guests use.

19

5 Finding out the house rules

Objectives

1 To help students understand and follow a landlady outlining the house rules.
2 To give students practice in reading the kinds of rules found in hotels.

Tape

Tapescript

Judy:	Well it's a lovely room. It's quite a nice size.
Landlady:	Oh yes. It's a good-sized room and it's well-furnished.
Judy:	Yes. Yes I can see that. Erm... is there anything that I should know?
Landlady:	Well, I don't allow the cat to go upstairs at all.
Judy:	Oh? Not at all.
Landlady:	No, absolutely not. I don't like cats upstairs (Oh right.) And I don't allow people to smoke in bedrooms.
Judy:	Oh no, no I agree with that. I don't smoke anyway.
Landlady:	And ...erm... I don't allow people to stick pictures up on the walls with sellotape. (Oh?) Well you see, when you take the picture down the sellotape leaves ...erm... a mark on the paper.
Judy:	Oh I see. Can I use blu-tack or something?
Landlady:	Oh yes. Something like that (Oh right) is quite acceptable. (Lovely) And there are just two more things (Oh) if you don't mind. (Yes.) If you do go out, would you please remember to close the window.
Judy:	Right. I'll do that.
Landlady:	And there's the kettle here, as you can see (Yes) but when you boil the kettle could you please put it on the floor and not on the chest of drawers?
Judy:	Oh I see. Does it make a mark or something?
Landlady:	Yes it would probably leave a mark.
Judy:	Oh right. I'll do that then.
Landlady:	Is...is that all right?
Judy:	Well it sounds very fair. Thank you very much.
Landlady:	Yes all right. (OK) Good.

Length: 1 min. 20 sec.
Number of speakers: 2.
Setting: A landlady is outlining the house rules to her new lodger.

20

Key language

Function: Telling someone what they can and cannot do.

Lexis: a good-sized room   a mark
   well-furnished   blu-tack
   upstairs   leave
   smoke (verb)   remember to...
   bedroom   kettle
   agree   boil
   stick   floor
   sellotape   chest of drawers

Structures: I don't allow...to do...
    If you do...could you do ...
    When you do...could you do...

TEACHING HINTS

While not much household vocabulary occurs on the tape, the picture in the Student's Book on page 10 could easily be used to teach some.

 To follow the tape and complete the task students do not need anything more than a passive understanding of the structures listed. These could either be explained through example before listening or left entirely (since their meaning is fairly self-evident on the tape).

Tasks

Before listening

Set the scene for the tape by asking students to compare their bedrooms with the one on page 10 in their books. Ask them to imagine the landlady of this room, for example, is she old-fashioned/modern, tidy/untidy etc.? Play a short extract from the tape to encourage this line of thinking. Try to help them to predict the kinds of house rules that might operate in this house by drawing their attention, for example, to the cat on the bed. Tell students they are going to hear a conversation between a new lodger and her landlady.

Listening task

While students are listening they should first locate the things mentioned on the tape, i.e. the kettle, the cat and so on. When they have spotted the key words their task is simply to mark with a cross the things prohibited and to make brief notes of the rules. Let them check their answers with each other and with you.

Reading task

Ask students to think back to when they were last guests in a hotel. Ask them to tell you some of the things guests need to know and do on arrival and on departure. Make two lists (one for arrival and one for departure) on the board. Then ask students to open their books at page 11 and to add anything they had

21

forgotten to the lists on the board. They should first read the information and check any unfamiliar words in the dictionary or with you.

Writing task

Check students' comprehension of the information they have read by asking them first to complete the 'on arrival' task and then complete the 'on departure' note. After each task encourage students to check their answers with each other. At the end of the lesson check that their answers are correct.

5 Finding out the house rules

Listening

Put a cross on the picture where the rule is being broken. Make brief notes of each rule.

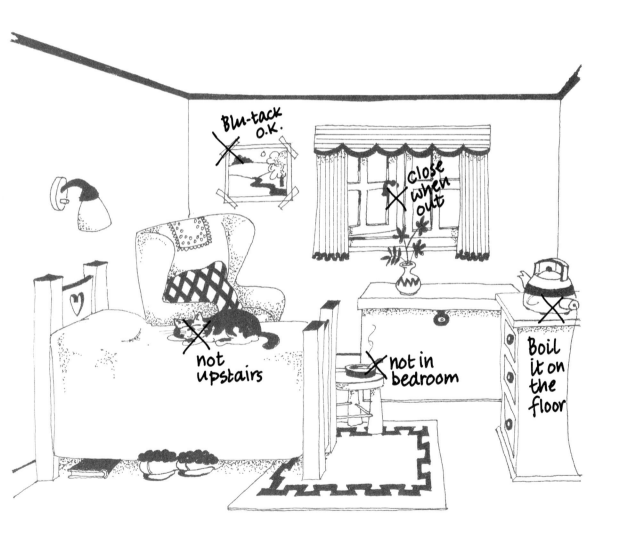

Reading and writing

You are staying at a hotel. Read the notices below.

On arrival Find your room. Put a circle round the number on the plan.
Find the fire exit. Put 'FE' on the plan and draw a line from your room to the exit.
Find the nearest fire extinguisher. Put a circle round the symbol on the plan.

On departure Pay bill for 7 nights = £ *105.00*

Where do I leave the key? *Reception*

Can I leave my room after lunch? *No. By noon.*

Can I pay by cheque? *with a banker's card.*

It is essential that all guests read this notice.

Fire Precautions

If you detect a fire
1. Sound the fire alarm.
2. For small local outbreaks, and if there is no personal danger, try to put out the fire by using the nearest extinguisher.

In the event of fire
1. Warning bells/sirens will ring continuously.
2. Close all doors and windows.
3. Evacuate the Hotel by using: —
your nearest exit, which is

TURN LEFT THEN RIGHT
. . . .
TO EXIT
. . . .

General Information

Vacating Rooms
Bedrooms must be vacated by NOON on the day of departure. PLEASE LEAVE YOUR KEY WITH RECEPTION.

Cheques
We regret that cheques cannot be accepted unless supported by a bankers card.

Your room number is	*14*

Your room rate is £ *15.00* per night
for *1* person

including morning paper, early morning tea, English breakfast and VAT.

Departure date	*7 August*

Key
★ - Fire Extinguisher
1, 2 etc. - bedroom numbers

9 10 11 12 13

8

7
6

4   5

3   2   1

14

15   BAR   RECEPTION

RESTAURANT

FE ★

MAIN ENTRANCE

24

6 Phoning a flat-owner

Objectives

1 To give students practice in understanding information given over the phone about accommodation.
2 To give students practice in reading and writing letters confirming the renting of accommodation.

Tape

Tapescript

Rod: Hello. Is that Oxford 40414?
Mary: Yes it is.
Rod: Erm... I'm enquiring about the flat which was advertised in the local paper.
Mary: Oh yes?
Rod: Wonder if you could tell me, how much is the rent a month, please?
Mary: It's £112.
Rod: I see. Is it fairly near the city centre?
Mary: Yes, it's only about a kilometre away.
Rod: I see. Is it quite handy for the shops?
Mary: Yes, within a minute or two on foot.
Rod: Good. What about a garden?
Mary: Well you have the use of the garden.
Rod: I see. And central heating, is there?
Mary: Yes, yes. Gas central heating.
Rod: I see. Erm... how many rooms are there, please?
Mary: Well, there's one very large bed-sitting room, a kitchen and bathroom and a small hall.
Rod: I see. Erm... which floor is it on?
Mary: On the first floor.
Rod: Oh good. Erm... would it be possible for me to visit it tomorrow, say about 5 o'clock?
Mary: Yes, certainly.
Rod: Oh good. That's fine. Could you just give me your name, please?
Mary: Yes. The name is Mary Jones (Yes) and the address is 41 North Parade.
Rod: 41 North Parade. Fine. Thanks ever so much. I'll see you tomorrow at 5 o'clock then.
Mary: Yes. (OK?) Good.

Rod: Byebye.
Mary: Goodbye.

Length: 1 min. 20 sec.
Number of speakers: 2.
Setting: A prospective tenant telephoning a flat-owner from a call box about a
        flat.

Key language

Function: Eliciting and giving information about a flat.

Lexis:	
rent	bed-sitting room
city centre	kitchen
handy for	bathroom
garden	hall
central heating	floor

Structures: I'm enquiring about...
            how much is...a month
            about a...away
            within a minute or two on foot
            you have the use of...
            there's...

TEACHING HINTS

Teach lexis and structures in the context of your school or college. Ask where
things are inside the college, e.g. 'Where's the language lab?' 'It's on the first
floor'. Then ask where places are in relation to the college, e.g. 'Where's the bus
stop?' 'It's a minute or two on foot.' For further practice, ask students to answer
questions about their own homes in a similar way.

Tasks

Before listening

Ask students what information they would want about a flat before they went to
see it. Compile a list of topics on the board, e.g. rent, number of rooms etc., and
briefly ask for details of the kind of thing they would like. Then ask students to
open their books at page 12 and look at the things Rod (who is looking for a flat
and has seen an advertisement in the newspaper) would like to know. Elicit the
number he is ringing. Do not present the flat-owner, as part of the task is to find
out her name. Set the scene for the tape: Rod is by the phone with his notes about
what to ask.

Listening task

Tell students that their task is to fill in the answers for Rod on the note pad. Let
them check their answers with each other then with you. Finally ask them if they
would be interested in renting the flat.

Reading task

Tell students that Rod has been to see the flat and that he likes it very much and has said so to Mary Jones, the owner. Ask them what he might do next and elicit or tell them that he is going to write to Ms Jones (Ms=Miss or Mrs) confirming in writing that he wishes to rent the flat for one year from the first of next month. Ask students to look at page 13 and explain that if they put the extracts from the four letters together, they will find a complete example of a letter of this type. Let them do this individually and silently. When the majority have achieved this, elicit the complete letter from various members of the class.

Writing task

Now ask students to complete the letter with the gaps for Rod Stevens. They can either do this in class or at home. Point out that this can serve as a model for them if ever they need to write an English letter of this type.

6 Phoning a flat-owner

Listening

Put a tick or a cross in the boxes.
Fill in the missing information.

> Ring Oxford 40414 about
> furnished flat
> Find out: ☑ or ☒
>   Near City Centre ☑
>   Near Shops ☑
>   Garden ☑
>   Central heating ☑
>   Visit tomorrow 5 p.m. ☑
>   Rent per month €112
>   Number of rooms 3
> Floor first
> Name of landlord/landlady
>   Mary Jones
> Address 41 North Parade

Reading and writing

Using the other letters and the information on the tape to help you, write to the landlady to say that you would like to rent her flat.

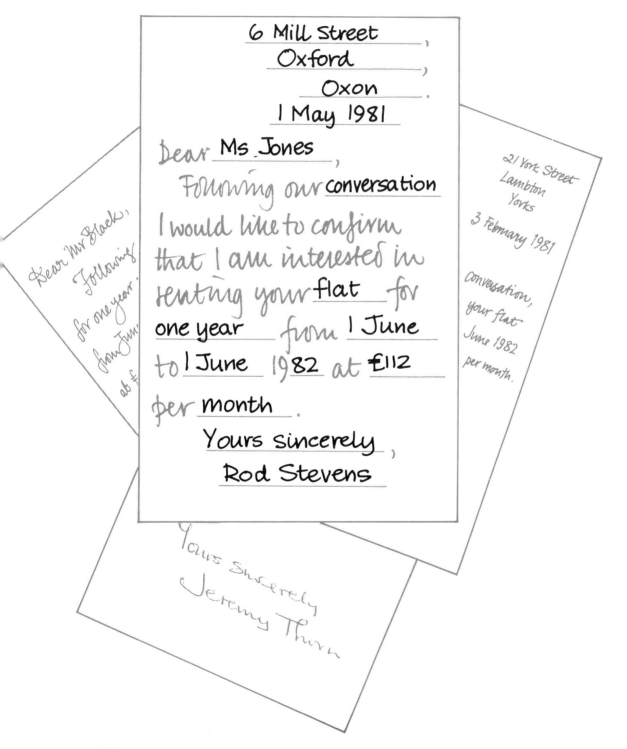

6 Mill Street ,
Oxford ,
Oxon .
1 May 1981

Dear Ms Jones ,
    Following our conversation
I would like to confirm
that I am interested in
renting your flat for
one year from 1 June
to 1 June 1982 at £112
per month .
    Yours sincerely ,
    Rod Stevens

Dear Mr Black ,
Following
for one year
from June
at

21 York Street
Lambton
Yorks

3 February 1981

conversation,
your flat
June 1982
per month.

Yours Sincerely
Jeremy Thorn

29

7 Using a bank account

Objectives

1 To give students practice in understanding simple instructions given by a bank cashier.
2 To give students practice in reading a bank statement and basic banking information.
3 To give students practice in writing a cheque and filling in a standing order form.

Tape

Tapescript

Alex: Good morning.

Cashier: Good morning.

Alex: I would... I would want to know how to make out this cheque.

Cashier: Right. Erm... do you want to draw out some money?

Alex: Yes, £20.

Cashier: £20 OK. (Yes) Well, the first thing you need to do, is to write today's date in the top right-hand corner where you see the line (Yes) at the top you write just today's date (Yes) and the year. You must put the year in. And if you want to draw out money after it says pay... can you see over on the left-hand side?

Alex: The first.. er... line?

Cashier: That's it. On the first line it says PAY and you write 'Cash' afterwards.

Alex: In letters.

Cashier: Yes. CASH (Yes) you write cash. OK. Then underneath that, right underneath, you have to write the amount of money you want. So just twenty pounds and then you write ONLY at the end in words. Then at the end of that line where you can see the box, see over on the right-hand side, you have to write the amount you want in numbers (In numbers?). Mm-mm. (Yes) And then underneath that box, the last thing you have to do in the bottom right-hand corner is just write your signature.

Alex: Thank you very much.

Cashier: OK. Byebye then.

Alex: Bye.

Length: 1 min. 25 sec.
Number of speakers: 2.
Setting: At the counter in a bank.

Key language

Function: Asking for and giving basic banking information.

Lexis:
make out
cheque
draw out
date
in the top/bottom right-hand corner
line

year
on the left-hand side
cash
amount
signature

Structures:
I want to know how to...
The first thing you need to do is to...
you write...
You must...
it says...and you...
underneath
you have to...
The last thing you have to do is...

TEACHING HINTS

Present the banking vocabulary in the context of paying for things, e.g. 'Cash is the money in your pocket. If you haven't got any, you can go to the bank to draw some out...or you can make out a cheque.' When these have been practised, present the structures and other lexical items necessary by drawing a letter on the board and teaching the layout, e.g. 'You put the address in the top right-hand corner.' You could also draw a picture with, perhaps, the sun in the top right-hand corner etc., and ask students to locate each item in the picture. Then ask them to give you instructions as to where to locate things in a picture of their own design, or an imaginary form of some kind.

Tasks

Before listening

Set the scene by telling students that Alex Other, a student whose English isn't very good, has gone into an English bank because he needs some cash. Tell them they are going to hear his conversation with a bank cashier. Revise banking vocabulary at this point. Ask students to guess what his problem is (how to make out an English cheque) or tell them that this is his problem. Tell them to open their books at page 14 and read the two cartoons with them. Elicit the fact that in England you can make out a cheque on anything, but advise them against it!

Listening task

Tell students that their task is to fill in the cheque for Alex. Let them check their answers with each other and then with you. Draw a large cheque on the board and tell them to instruct you as to how to make it out for Alex. A possible follow-up would be to ask students to bring to the next lesson a cheque made out on something unusual. These can then be used to decorate the classroom.

Reading task

Present 'statement', 'in the black' and 'in the red/overdrawn'. Do not discuss students' own bank statements if they might be embarrassed or offended. Tell them that Alex is a good client and isn't in the red. Ask them to look at the statement on page 15. Let them guess what tells you that Alex is in the black ('C' after each balance) and what would show he was in the red ('D' after each balance). Ask them to work out which column shows money coming into the account and thus to deduce the meaning of the headings 'Credit' and 'Debit'. Tell them that the numbers on the left of the second column are his cheque numbers and explain that credit transfer means that someone has paid money into his account. Then ask them to read the extract on standing orders, asking you or using a good dictionary to help with any unfamiliar words. To check their understanding, ask if you can pay for a meal by standing order, or if you can pay your rent with one. Finally, go through the statement column by column, checking that everything is clear and ask how much Alex has in the account at this moment (£51.72). Then let the students do the task first (Alex can only afford television A).

Writing task

Go through the standing order form answering any questions. Tell the class that Alex wants to pay for his new television every month by standing order and so they must fill in the form for him. Go through it orally first, eliciting what must be written and then ask students to fill in the form either in class or for homework.

32

Listening

Fill in the blank cheque according to the instructions given by the bank cashier.

A man once wrote one on an egg, and it was cashed.

1 May 19 81   40-18-40

Midland Bank Limited

143 Radford Road
Radford Coventry Warwickshire CV6 3BS

or order

£ 20 ———— 00

A·N·OTHER

Pay Cash

Twenty pounds only

A. N. Other

Specimen

"573054" 40"1840": 0064391211"

Another man wrote one on a cow, but that was rather more difficult.

Reading and writing

Which television can Mr A. N. Other afford to buy?
He wants to make the hire purchase payments by standing order. Fill in the form
for him. The TV shop, Jackson's Ltd, also banks with the Midland Bank in
Coventry. Their account number is 00456823.

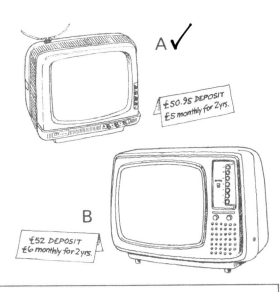

A ✓

£50.95 DEPOSIT
£5 monthly for 2yrs.

B

£52 DEPOSIT
£6 monthly for 2yrs.

£57 DEPOSIT
£7 monthly for 2yrs.

C

Midland Bank Limited
143 RADFORD ROAD
RADFORD COVENTRY WARWICKS CV6 3BS

A N OTHER ESQ

Statement of Account

1977	SHEET 001 ACCOUNT NO 00643912	DEBIT	CREDIT	BALANCE	Credit C Debit D
FEB16	CREDIT TRANSFER		21.55	21.55	C
FEB17	100231	15.00		6.55	C
FEB23	STANDING ORDER	2.56		3.99	C
FEB28	CREDIT TRANSFER		21.26	25.25	C
MAR 2	100233	12.00		13.25	C
MAR 3	100232	7.00		6.25	C
MAR 7	STANDING ORDER	2.56		3.69	C
MAR 8	CREDIT TRANSFER		30.64	34.33	C
MAR 8	100234	10.00		24.33	C
MAR 9	STANDING ORDER	2.56		21.77	C
MAR11	CREDIT TRANSFER		25.96	47.73	C
MAR17	100235	15.00		32.73	C
MAR23	STANDING ORDER	2.56		30.17	C
MAR24	CREDIT TRANSFER		21.55	51.72	C
MAR29	BALANCE CARRIED FORWARD			51.72	C

Standing Order Mandate

TO **MIDLAND** _____ Bank Limited   Date **(today's date)**
Address **143 Radford Road, Coventry, Warwicks, CV6 3BS**

Please pay

Bank	Branch Title not address	Sorting Code number
MIDLAND	**COVENTRY**	**40-18-40**

for the credit of

Beneficiary	Account number
JACKSON'S LTD	**00456823**

†the sum of

Amount in figures	Amount in words
£ **5.00**	**Five pounds**

commencing

Date and amount of first payment		Date and frequency
~~Now~~ **(date)** £ **5.00**	and thereafter every	**(date) every month**

until

Date and amount of last payment	
£ **5.00**	*until you receive further notice from me/us in writing

quoting the reference   and debit my/our account accordingly.

*This instruction cancels any previous order in favour of the beneficiary named above, under this reference.
*Delete as appropriate
†If the amounts of periodic payments vary they should be incorporated in a schedule overleaf.

Special instructions

Signature/s   **A. N. Other**

Title of account and account number to be debited   **A. N. OTHER ESQ.**   **00643912**

Note: The Bank will not undertake to
a) make any reference to Value Added Tax or pay a stated sum plus V.A.T.
b) advise remitter's address to beneficiary.
c) advise beneficiary of inability to pay.
d) request beneficiary's banker to advise beneficiary of receipt.

Standing orders and direct debiting are just two of the services available when you have a current account.
With a standing order you tell us about regular bills of a fixed amount like rent, rates and H.P. payment, and we remember to pay them out of your money. You just sign a form like the one shown here.

8 Leaving a message

Objectives

1 To give students practice in taking telephone messages.
2 To give students practice in reading notices and writing messages.

Tape

Tapescript

Fiona:	Hello.
Stuart:	Hello.
Fiona:	Oh. Is that Stuart?
Stuart:	Yes.
Fiona:	Hello Stuart, it's Fiona.
Stuart:	Oh. Hi Fiona.
Fiona:	Hi. Erm... is Judy there by any chance?
Stuart:	No I'm sorry she's just popped out to the shops.
Fiona:	Oh dear. Erm... could you possibly leave a message?
Stuart:	Yes. Yes. Just a second, let me get a piece...bit of paper.
Fiona:	Thank you.
Stuart:	OK.
Fiona:	Er... the thing is we've arranged to play tennis this afternoon (Mm-mm) at 3 o'clock (Yes) ...erm... but I've got a problem because the string on my racquet's broken (Mm-mm) but I think that Judy's got an extra racquet (Yes I think she has) and so I was wondering if you could ask her to bring the extra one along.
Stuart:	Yes. OK. I'll do that.
Fiona:	OK and ...er... oh yes one other thing. She borrowed a book from me (Mm-mm) and I think she's probably forgotten all about it. I wonder if you could possibly remind her to bring that along as well.
Stuart:	She knows what it is, does she?
Fiona:	Yes, yes. It's a novel.
Stuart:	Yes. OK. So bring extra racquet and ...er... the book that she borrowed.
Fiona:	That's right. (OK) 3 o'clock.
Stuart:	I'll tell her.
Fiona:	Thanks very much, Stu.
Stuart:	OK. Cheerio.
Fiona:	Bye.
Stuart:	Bye.

Length: 1 min. 18 sec.
Number of speakers: 2.
Setting: Someone is ringing a friend who is out so she has to leave a message.

Key language

Function: Leaving telephone messages.

Lexis:
tennis	arranged to do
(extra) racquet	bring something along
string	borrow
broken	forget
this afternoon	remind someone
at 3 o'clock	as well
popped out	a novel
leave a message	

Structures: Is that ...?
It's Fiona
Is Judy there?
I'm sorry she's (popped) out
Could you possibly ...?
I was wondering if you could ...?
I wonder if you could possibly ...?

TEACHING HINTS

Very little of the above needs to be in the students' active vocabulary for them to be able to follow what is going on on the tape and complete the task. However the tape could very usefully reinforce some earlier introduction to 'telephone language'. It is impossible to predict the language needed to leave telephone messages but a simple framework can be given on which students can build, something along the lines of:

A: Bath 55677.
B: Hello. Is that Peter? This is Kay.
A: Hello Kay.
B: Is Paul in?
A: No. He's out at the moment.
B: Oh. Can you leave him a message for me?
A: Yes, of course.
B: Could you possibly tell him...
A: Ok. I'll leave a note for him.
B: Thanks a lot. Bye.

If you wanted to practise writing messages then students could decide, individually, the message they want to leave. Then in pairs, sitting back to back in order to simulate telephone conditions, they could have a conversation leaving a message. The receiver of the message would then actually write it.

Tasks

Before listening

Tell the students they are going to hear someone leaving a message over the phone. If you think your students will find the tape difficult you may want to prepare them further by drawing their attention to page 16 in the Student's Book and looking for the differences between the four drawings. In this way they will realise that the items to listen for are time and what she asks her friend to bring with her.

Listening task

Tell students to look at the drawing and decide which one best represents the message. Let them check their answers with each other then with you.

Reading task

The notices and messages on page 17 have been chosen to give students an idea of the range of this kind of writing.

Students should first tackle the reading by looking at each of the notices and trying to work out what the unfamiliar words mean. Of course it is impossible to deduce the meaning of Labrador but draw students' attention to its position in the sentence, i.e. before the noun, and its capital letter and help them come to the conclusion that it probably has something to do with the type of dog. This approach to unfamiliar vocabulary should be encouraged so that eventually students will try to make reasoned guesses before seizing their dictionaries.

The next stage is to decide where these notices would be seen. If students find this difficult put a list of possible places on the board for them to choose from.

Writing task

Before doing the writing discuss with students the kind of information that should be included. This list might include the time the note was left, where the writer had gone and where the key could be found, e.g. with the nextdoor neighbour, under the mat. It would also be necessary to point out how this kind of writing differs from other kinds, i.e. that personal pronouns, articles, auxiliary verbs, and conjunctions are omitted.

8   Leaving a message

Listening

Which picture best represents the message?
Put a tick beside the correct one.

Reading and writing

Where would you expect to see these notices?

Completed writing task

WANTED

GOOD HOMES for Labrador Puppies 7 weeks old.

Tel : 96701

Shop window

FOR SALE
Slazenger tennis racquet, hardly used. £8 o.n.o.
Tel 55944

Shop window

3 PINTS TODAY PLEASE

Front door step

LONDON

COACH FOR LONDON
LEAVES SCHOOL AT 8 A.M.
SATURDAY
DON'T BE LATE.

School/college notice board

CAR PARK FULL

Entrance to car park

CLOSED
FOR LUNCH 1–2.15

Shop door

JOHN
Gone to work!
Milk, butter in fridge.
Cornflakes, bread, jam in cupboard. Help yourself!
See you later.
Peter.

kitchen table

You have to go out for half an hour.
Write a message to leave on your door for a friend who is arriving today.

9.30.
Gone out. Be back at 10.00.

Key with next door No. 25.

Make yourself at home.

Jason

9 Learning how to use a machine

Objectives

1 To help students understand and follow someone giving instructions about the use of a machine.
2 To give students practice in reading and writing instructions.

Tape

Tapescript

Jackie:	OK. The washing machine, look, is next to the fridge, here.
Yumiko:	Yes.
Jackie:	Erm...have you used one like this before?
Yumiko:	Yes, I have.
Jackie:	OK. Now, what d'you need to know? Let's see. Erm...obviously you put the clothes in here in this compartment here. (In here) And you open the door (Yes) yes. One thing to remember about this machine – when you close the door, you have to close it quite firmly (Mm-mm) because it's stiff.
Yumiko:	Ah, it's stiff, yes.
Jackie:	OK? (Mm-mm) Erm...what else? The powder. You need to put the washing powder (Mm-mm) in this drawer here.
Yumiko:	So? (Mm-mm) Er...which compartment do I have to put it in?
Jackie:	Er...put it in the middle one, (Mm-mm) in the middle.
Yumiko:	How much...how much washing powder do I need?
Jackie:	About a cupful. (Mm-mm) OK? (Yes) So, close up the drawer... that's fine. (Mm) Er...what other dials have we got here? The dial on the end here (Yes) is the programme setter. (Uh-huh) OK? Usually, if you're washing white clothes, (Mm) you set this dial to number 2. (Right) OK? (Yes) Is there anything else you need to know?
Yumiko:	Er...what about temperature?
Jackie:	Oh yes, you can vary the temperature on this one too. Erm... if you're washing woollens, you turn the temperature dial right down to minimum.
Yumiko:	All round, mm.
Jackie:	Mm-mm. And, of course, if you're washing things like towels (Mm-mm) or white sheets, turn it up to maximum.
Yumiko:	Maximum is very hot? (Yes) Ah, yes.
Jackie:	OK. Erm...is there anything else?
Yumiko:	And then I have to turn on...

Jackie: Turn on here. (Mm-mm) That's it...and the red light comes on.
Yumiko: Ah, I see. And, erm...turn it on at the wall?
Jackie: Yes, obviously. (Yes) It's over there (Mm) just behind the fridge. You
          can see the switch. (Yes) Turn it on there.
Yumiko: Uh-huh. And how long does it take?

Length: 2 min. 3 sec.
Number of speakers: 2.
Setting: A young housewife talking to her au pair in the kitchen.

Key language

Function: Showing how to use a washing machine.

Lexis: washing machine   drawer
         clothes   cupful
         woollens   temperature
         towels   dial
         sheets   maximum
         washing powder   minimum
         compartment   programme setter
         middle   on/off control

Structures: you have to...
              you need to...
              you put ... in here
              you set...
              next to...
              on the end
              over there
              behind...

TEACHING HINTS

The structures can be presented in any setting where someone is showing
someone else how to do something. The classroom situation obviously limits your
choice of the 'something'. If you are teaching a multi-lingual class and have a
Japanese student then it could be Origami, the art of paper folding. Some
students might know how to play Noughts and Crosses or Hangman and could
tell the others how to play. Play the game a couple of times using the structures as
appropriate. Now ask students to write an explanation of the game. They could
do this individually or in groups or the class could make suggestions and you
compile the explanation on the board. Ask students to look at page 18 in their
books. Use the diagram of the machine to teach the key lexis.

Tasks

Before listening

Tell students they are going to hear someone being shown how to use a washing
machine. Many will have used a machine like this and will be able to tell you the
purpose of the dials and drawer on the control panel. Some might feel that

washing machines are 'only for women'. If so, you may be able to keep their interest by dwelling more on lexis such as automation, computer programmes, control panels and so on. Reassure them by pointing out that the aim is not to learn how to use a washing machine but to practise following instructions.

Listening task

Tell students to listen in order to find out the purpose of the three dials on the control panel. Ask them to label them. Then tell them to listen again to find out the control settings for washing sheets and towels and to mark each of these with an arrow on the dials. Finally, tell students to listen again to find out where the clothes and washing powder go and how much powder to use. Let them check their answers with each other then with you.

Reading task

Ask students to look at the picture on page 19 in their books. Before reading ask questions to help them explain how the machine works, e.g. 'What is coming out of the tap?' 'What are the bells for?' You can feed in a lot of the more difficult vocabulary from the passage during this part of the lesson. Now tell students to read the passage. You could ask them to indicate the function of each part of the machine. This would encourage a closer reading.

Writing task

Having done the reading task students should understand fairly well how the machine works. Ask them to say what instructions they would give to someone who was going to navigate this machine for the first time. If they can do this ask them to write the instructions using the key words in their book. The key words are intended only as a guide. If your students are capable of writing fuller instructions, encourage them to do so.

Listening

Label the three dials and use arrows to show their settings for washing white sheets and towels. Mark where the powder is put and note how much to use.

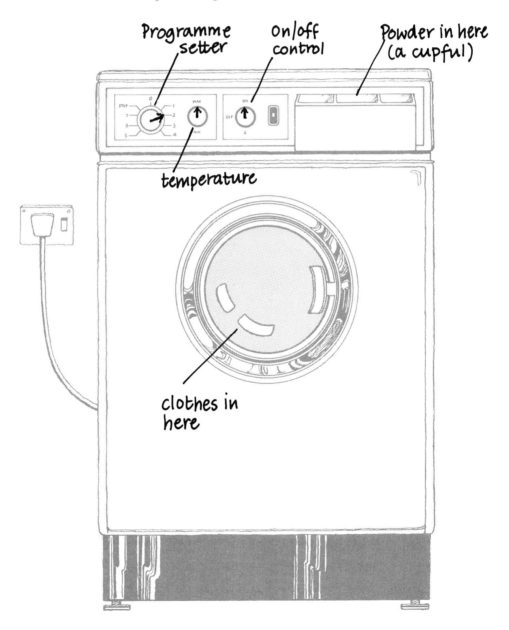

Programme setter

On/off control

Powder in here (a cupful)

temperature

clothes in here

The Anti-Litter Machine

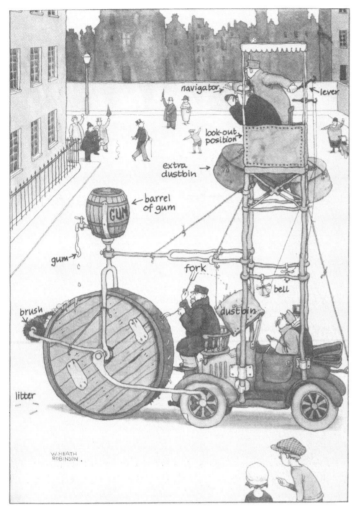

The mechanism is simple.
A barrel of gum drips slowly onto a large wooden wheel and a brush evenly distributes the sticky substance over the wheel. Cigarette ends and other litter stick to the wheel as the motor car drives it over the road. Behind the wheel sits one of the operators who picks the litter off with forks and deposits it behind him in a dustbin. The dustbin is replaced by one of the other three when full.

Above the motor car is a look-out position where the two navigators stand. They look for litter and direct the car towards it. This is done via a system of levers and bells. The upper lever rings the bell on the left of the driver which directs him to the right, and the lower lever rings the bell on the right which directs him to the left.

Write the instructions you would give to someone taking the job of navigator for the first time. Use the key words to help you.

Key words   1 Stand/look-out position   3 Turn right/upper lever
2 See/litter/direct car   4 Turn left/lower lever

> You stand in the look-out position and when you see some litter in the road you direct the car towards it. If you want to turn right you push the upper lever; if you want to turn left you push the lower lever.

10 Finding the way

Objectives

1 To help students understand and follow directions given to a motorist over the phone.
2 To give students practice in sifting out information relevant to a specific journey, from maps and charts, and in using this information to write directions.

Tape

Tapescript

Jackie: 99522. Hello.
Fiona: Hello Jackie!
Jackie: Fiona! Where are you?
Fiona: Oh, ah, dear! I seem to have got lost.
Jackie: Oh!
Fiona: Well, I mean, not completely lost. I am in Oxford.
Jackie: Oh well done! Well done!
Fiona: I think I am, anyway.
Jackie: Er...whereabouts?
Fiona: Well, erm...near the Polytechnic. You see, I came down the London Road (Uh-huh) through Headington (Uh-huh) and then I turned left (Uh-huh) and then I found the Polytechnic and there's a phone box here (Ah) and I'm facing it now...
Jackie: Yes (if you see what I mean) I think I know where you are. (Mm-mm) I know where you are. Erm...well, you've gone completely the wrong way.
Fiona: Oh no, have I? (Yes, yes) Oh dear.
Jackie: Erm...the best thing to do is to turn round and go back to the London Road.
Fiona: Oh...the way I came?
Jackie: That's right, to the roundabout.
Fiona: So I go back through Headington, yes...
Jackie: Yes, to the roundabout. That's where you came off the M40, in fact.
Fiona: That's right, yes.
Jackie: OK. Well, take the first exit on the left...
Fiona: The first exit on the left.
Jackie: At the roundabout there...
Fiona: Uh-huh.

Jackie: And it's a dual carriageway. (Mm-mm) It's all part of the ring road that goes round the city.

Fiona: Oh yes, I see (OK) OK.

Jackie: So you go along the by-pass (Mm) erm...until you come to the next roundabout (Mm) and at that roundabout, go straight across.

Fiona: Yes.

Jackie: All right, then go on a bit further – it's not far – and then you'll come to yet another roundabout. (Mm-mm) Now that's the third roundabout. (OK) All right? (Yes) And there you take the second exit on the left.

Fiona: OK.

Jackie: And this is quite a small road. It's called Godstow Road. (Godstow Road) Yes. (Right) And you go down that road, (Mm-mm) over a bridge and (Yes) our road is the second on the left after the bridge.

Fiona: OK, so over the bridge (Mm-mm) and then second on the left.

Jackie: Uh-huh. OK. I'll put some coffee on.

Fiona: Oh lovely.

Jackie: See you soon.

Fiona: Bless you! OK. See you later.

Jackie: Bye.

Fiona: Bye.

Length: 1 min. 59 sec.
Number of speakers: 2.
Setting: Lost motorist phones friend for directions.

Key language

Function: Asking for and giving directions.

Lexis:

get lost	dual carriageway
whereabouts	ring road
phone box	by-pass
roundabout	not far
Polytechnic	bridge
M40	further
exit	

Structures:

I came down...	take ...
I turned left...	on the left
I found the Polytechnic...	go along...
near...	...until
facing...	you come to...
over...	go straight across
turn round	go on...
go back to...	

TEACHING HINTS

All the structures are used on the tape to say where you are, how you got there, and how to get somewhere else. These structures can be explained and practised using very simple diagrams on the board. For further practice everyone would need to have a copy of a map. Pick a point on the map and tell the students how you got there and see if they can 'find' you. Then give directions to another place and see if they can follow you. This can be repeated but instead of you giving directions students could do this in pairs.

The teaching of the key lexis should present few problems. You may want to teach a number of other items as well which fit into this vocabulary field, e.g. traffic lights, speed limit, road sign. On one side of the board draw pictures of the things you want students to learn, not in any great detail but recognisable, and on the other side write the words. Tell students to look up these words in a dictionary and then to match the words with the pictures.

Tasks

Before listening

Ask students to have a look at the map on page 20 in their books. Tell them what a canal is and point out the symbol for roundabouts. Tell them they are going to hear a conversation between someone in a phone box who has lost her way and her friend who is at home.

Listening task

Tell students to listen first in order to find out the position of the phone box and to mark it with a cross on the map. Check that everyone has their cross in the right place before going on. Now ask them to listen to the directions given to the girl in the phone box, Fiona, and to follow them to find her friend's house. Ask them to trace the route on the map. Play the tape as many times as is necessary to get them all to Fiona's destination. Let them check their answers together and with you.

Reading task

Students may already have asked what M40 stands for and in the legend on page 21 in their books they can see the other classes of roads. The map in conjunction with the legend is fairly self-evident, given time. The mileage table is an easy way of finding the distance by road between two places. The distance between Lincoln and Norwich, for example, can be found by moving vertically down from 'Lincoln' and horizontally across from 'Norwich'. The number written at the point here these two meet is the distance, in this case 106 miles.

Writing task

Ask students to ring Groby and Stapleford on the map and then jot down the roads that connect them. Write the following structures on the board:
take the ... to ...
join the motorway at junction ...
leave the motorway at junction ...

Now ask them to give you oral directions from Groby to Stapleford, checking that they are using the above structures as necessary. When they have done this ask them to write the directions in the space provided.

Listening

Mark the position of the call box with a cross.
Trace the route to Fiona's friend's house on the map.

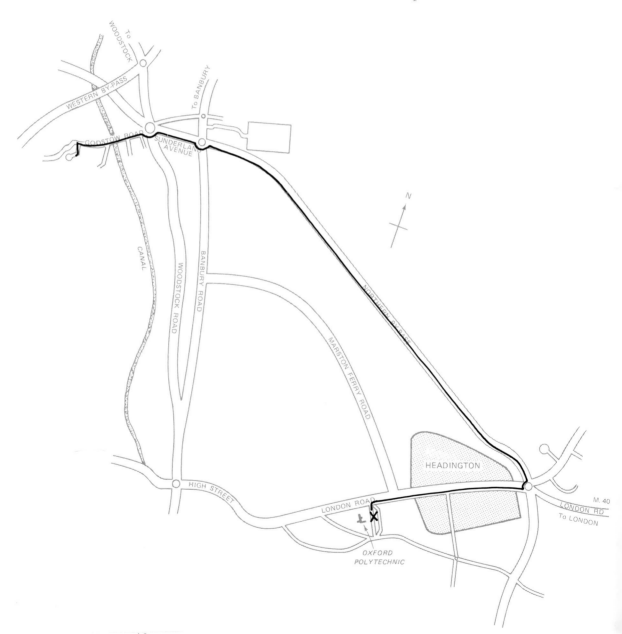

M1 LEICESTER - ALFRETON

Mileages

Hull	Inverness	Kendal	Leeds	Leicester	Lincoln	Liverpool	Manchester	Newcastle upon Tyne	Norwich	Nottingham	Oxford
378											
124	294										
55	347	71									
87	436	160	96								
37	406	138	67	51							
128	368	73	73	107	118						
93	367	73	40	87	84	35					
117	262	85	92	181	151	154	129				
143	512	244	173	118	106	215	184	257			
73	411	137	67	25	36	97	70	156	124		
156	505	212	160	69	119	154	142	250	139	94	

Using the information from a motoring handbook, write directions for someone driving from Groby (near Leicester) to Stapleford (near Nottingham).

Take the A50 to Coalville.
Join the M1 at junction 22.
Leave the motorway at
junction 25. Take the
A52 to Stapleford.

Legend

Motorway open with junction numbers ══3══	Service areas open ⊗
A roads ──A6──	Airport ✈
B roads ─B5248─	
Unclassified roads ═══	

Completed writing task

11 Enquiring about a course

Objectives

1 To help students understand and follow someone giving information about dates, numbers and prices.
2 To give students practice in reading job advertisements and in sifting out information necessary to choose the best job for the profile given.

Tape

Tapescript

Receptionist: Good morning. Can I help you?
Student: Yes please. I would want to have some information about the ...erm... the courses at Swan School.
Receptionist: Is that a summer course you're interested in?
Student: Yes. Yes, please.
Receptionist: Yes. Fine. OK. Well, we have ...erm... short intensive full-time courses during the summer.
Student: Mm-mm. I would want to know the length of one course.
Receptionist: Yes. Each course lasts for three weeks.
Student: How many hours per week, please?
Receptionist: Well, it's about twenty-three hours a week. Usually four and a half days each week.
Student: You must have a lot of students in the class, haven't you?
Receptionist: We have a lot of students in the school but in the classes only about between twelve and fourteen students.
Student: Twelve and fourteen. Could you please give me the dates of the first and the second course?
Receptionist: Yes, certainly. The first course begins on 3 July and lasts until 20 July and the second course is from 24 July until 10 August.
Student: What about the fees per course?
Receptionist: Yes, each... each course costs £150 plus VAT, which is 15 per cent, and a £5 registration fee.
Student: And deposit, please?
Receptionist: Yes, for each course we need a deposit of £20 and the £5 registration fee.
Student: Oh thank you. Do we have to find our ...our own accommodation?
Receptionist: No, we can do that for you. We have a lady who arranges the accommodation for you with Oxford families.
Student: How much does it cost?

50

Receptionist: Well, you can choose to have bed and breakfast only which is £20 a week, or bed, breakfast and dinner which is about £27 a week.
Student: £27. Thank you very much.
Receptionist: You're welcome.

Length: 1 min. 47 sec.
Number of speakers: 2.
Setting: In the school office.

Key language

Function: Asking for and giving information about duration, price and number.

Lexis:

course	registration
length	fee
hours	plus
students	VAT
class	deposit
school	accommodation
dates	bed
first	breakfast
second	dinner

Structures:
... lasts for ...
how many ...?
per week
... a week
begins on ...
lasts until...
... is from...

TEACHING HINTS

The structures are all ways of expressing duration and frequency and so can be presented and practised in any context where these two notions occur, e.g. enquiring about theatre programmes, interviewing a sportsman about his training programme. If you decide to use the second suggestion choose a sportsman in a sport which most of your students are interested in, or alternatively a sport which is in some way topical. Ask what the students imagine a day in his life is like. Write their suggestions on the board. Ask them to think about how many hours a day he spends doing these various activities, what time he begins and finishes, how many times a week he trains, how long the season lasts, how long his career will last and so on. Encourage them to think about the frequency and the duration. You could go further and develop this into a role play where some students take the role of keen fans, young, budding sportsmen, reporters, school physical education teachers, and some the role of famous sportsman, coach, manager, trainer, sportsman's wife/mother/father. Tell the first group to write down the kinds of things they would like to find out from the sportsman and his 'managerial team'. Tell the second group to decide on details of the training programme and their individual parts in the sportsman's success. Now bring the two groups together for an interview session. If you feel this would not give your students enough guidance you could make out role cards with outlines of topics for them to ask about.

Tasks

Before listening

Ask students to look at the memo on page 22 in their books. Go through the questions and check students understand the vocabulary. When you come to the question 'How much' teach deposit, registration, fees and VAT. VAT stands for value added tax and the rate at the moment is 15 per cent.

Listening task

Play the tape once and ask students some context questions, e.g. 'Where are they?' 'Are they both English?' Establish who Peter is. Then ask students to listen again and to jot down the answers to Peter's questions on the memo. Play the tape as many times as necessary. Let students check their answers with each other then with you. Round off the lesson by asking if any of the students have been on an English language course before and if so how it compared with the one Peter is enquiring about.

Reading and writing tasks

The reading has little to do with courses, but just as Peter was finding out about courses to find the one which best suited him, so here the student is reading various job advertisements in order to find the one which best suits Mrs Starling. Ask students to open their books at page 23 and to underline anything they do not understand. Encourage them to suggest possible meanings for this lexis. By asking students questions you can direct them towards the meaning and an explanation arrived at in this way is often more memorable. Of course it can take a long time too. Now ask students to look at Mrs Starling's picture and read her advertisement and decide on the implications of having two children of school age. Point out that in England the school day is usually from 9 to 3.30 or 4 and the summer holiday is about six weeks, and that shop hours are usually 9 to 5.30. To help students decide on the best job for Mrs Starling ask them to note the advantages and disadvantages the jobs advertised in the grid. It might be a good idea to do the first one 'Store Detective' together. When they have filled in the grid the final stage is to transfer the noted advantages and disadvantages of the chosen job into a short paragraph in the space provided.

Listening

Write down the answers to Peter's questions.

Peter

dont forget to enquire about

ENGLISH LANGUAGE COURSES - TODAY!

Remember to ask :

How long ? 3 weeks

Dates? 3-20 July
24 July – 10 August

How many hours ? 23 hours 4½ days

How many students in class ? 12-14

How much ? £150 + V.A.T (15%) + £5 registration

Deposit ? £20

Accommodation

How much for:

Bed and breakfast £20.00

Bed and breakfast and dinner £27.00

Note the advantages and disadvantages of these five jobs for Mrs Starling.

VACANCIES

Store Detective

for FINGALS Department Store.
No previous experience
required. 40 hours per week.
TUES.– SAT. 9 a.m.– 5.30 p.m.
Apply: Mr Jones, Store
Personnel Manager, FINGALS,
LUTON

Home Help Wanted

6 hours p.w. Mon. Wed. Fri.
Hours to suit. £1.50 per hour (no
heavy work).
Write to: Mrs P. Johnson, 71
North St Luton

Receptionist/ Secretary

If you are an experienced
secretary with good speeds and a
pleasant friendly manner then
we have a job for you.
TOWERS Hotel is looking for a
receptionist to work 8 a.m.–2
p.m. daily. (1 weekend in 3 free)
£50 p.w. basic.
If you're interested ring us on
Luton 73371

Fashion

TREND fashion shop requires
part-time assistant to work
mornings only. MON.– FRI. 9
a.m.–1 p.m. 3 weeks paid
holiday.
Apply to: TREND, The High
Street, Luton

School meals Supervisor

Waynebridge First School
requires a canteen supervisor
starting in September. Hours 11
a.m.– 3 p.m. during school
terms.
Apply to: Education Division,
Town Hall, Luton

Job Wanted

Woman, two children of school
age, seeks employment. Good
typing and shorthand speeds.
Clean driving licence.
Tel: Luton 534674. Mrs Starling

Job	Advantages	Disadvantages
STORE DETECTIVE	No experience required	Hours: 9-5.30 Work Saturday
HOME HELP	Hours to suit	Not many hours
RECEPTIONIST/ SECRETARY	Good money. Hours quite good	Work 2 weekends in 3. 8 a.m bit early
SHOP ASSISTANT	Good hours	3 weeks holiday only
SCHOOL MEALS SUPERVISOR	Good hours School holidays	

Using the above say which job is most suitable for
Mrs Starling and why.

The best job for her is school meals
supervisor because she will work
when the children are at school
and will have the same holidays
as them.

54

Objectives

1　To give students practice in listening to someone making enquiries about hiring a car over the phone and in sifting out specific details.
2　To give students practice in reading information about road accidents presented in three different ways (in the form of a street plan, a graph and a formal description), and then to write a brief account of the accident shown.

Tape

Tapescript

Salesman:　773141.
Customer:　Oh hello, is that Self Drive Car Hire?
Salesman:　Yes, speaking. Can I help you?
Customer:　Oh yes, please. Erm... I wanted to enquire about hiring a car for the weekend.
Salesman:　Mm-mm. Yes. Well we do have special weekend rates, in fact, so... what kind of car would you like to have?
Customer:　Well it's... I'm not sure. Erm... what would be the best kind for a family of four... erm... plus space for camping equipment? We're going on a camping holiday.
Salesman:　Yes. I would think you would need something like an Allegro or Marina Estate or perhaps a Maxi. (I see) That'd be best I think.
Customer:　Yes. Erm...we'd be leaving on Friday, that's Friday July 7th (Yes) and returning on the Monday (Yes) that's...that's July 10th.
Salesman:　Yes, that's fine provided you pick up the car after 4 o'clock on the Friday and return it by 10 o'clock on the Monday.
Customer:　Ah-ha. I have to pick it up after 4 on Friday but return it before 10 (That's right) on Monday. (Yes) I see. Erm... could you tell me the basic cost?
Salesman:　It's £29.25 (Mm-mm) and the first three hundred miles are free but after that you have to pay $5\frac{1}{2}$p per mile.
Customer:　So that's $5\frac{1}{2}$p extra (Mm-mm) after the first three hundred miles.
Salesman:　Over three hundred miles yes (I see) and £29.25.
Customer:　Right thank you. Erm... is there...is it any extra for two drivers because my husband might want to drive as well?
Salesman:　Yes we do charge an extra £2.50 for each extra driver.
Customer:　I see. OK. Erm... and what about...er... VAT. Is that included?

Salesman: No I'm afraid that's not included. You'd have to add VAT at 15 per
cent to that price.
Customer: Mm-mm. Er... what about insurance? Is that included in the cost?
Salesman: Yes, yes, that's all included.
Customer: I see. OK thank you very much indeed.
Salesman: OK. Pleasure.
Customer: Byebye.
Salesman: Byebye.

Length: 1 min. 59 sec.
Number of speakers: 2.
Setting: On the phone to a car hire company.

Key language

Function: Asking for and giving information about car hire.

Lexis:

hire a car	return
weekend	by
kind (of car)	basic cost
space	free
camping equipment	extra
Allegro	drivers
Marina	charge
Maxi	VAT
Estate	include
pick up	insurance
after	

Structures: Could you tell me ...?
Is it any extra for...?
Is ... included?
...per mile

TEACHING HINTS

Begin by showing students pictures of different kinds of cars, e.g. estates, saloons, and different makes, e.g. Mini, Fiat 126. Show the students two pictures, one of a salesman and one of a young car buyer. Ask students to suggest the best kind of car for the young buyer. Then ask them to suggest the kinds of questions the buyer would ask the salesman. Write these on the board. Now ask them to suggest the kinds of answers he might receive. Write these on the board. While doing this introduce parts of the key language as appropriate. Underline the key language used in the questions and answers on the board.

Tasks

Before listening

Ask students who have cars to estimate roughly how much they cost a week to run. Then ask them to say how much, in their experience, cars cost to hire. Try to get them to think how the car hire companies arrive at the cost. Ask students to look at the handwritten list of questions on page 24 in their books. Give them a minute or two to read them and ask if there are any problems with the vocabulary. Tell them that they are going to hear someone phoning a car hire company.

Listening task

Tell students that their task is to write down the answers to the questions and that their answers need only be very brief. The question about the deposit has been included to encourage students to listen again in case they have missed something. Let them check their answers with each other then with you.

Reading task

Before starting to read anything ask students if they know the procedure to follow when involved in a road accident in their country. Suggest things to think about such as first aid, informing the police. Make a list of the suggestions they make. Now ask them to read 'What to do if involved in a road accident' on page 25 in their books. Deal with any items that need explanation and ask general questions to check comprehension. Now ask them to look at the graph. Explain what the two axes refer to and how conclusions can be drawn from the graph. This exercise could usefully follow some earlier work on comparatives.

Writing task

Before starting to write, remind students that in England we drive on the left. Check that they understand 'Halt sign' and 'Pedestrian witness'. Let students study the map for a few minutes and then ask questions to make sure everyone can visualise the accident. Ask students what information should go in the report and write headings on the board, e.g. time, position of witness, which direction car A was travelling in, the speed of the car. You can make these headings as full as you like depending on the amount of guidance your students need.

Listening

Write down the answers to the customer's questions.

CAR HIRE

Self drive- tel: 773141

Leave Friday 7 July and return Monday 10 July.

Things to find out:

Best kind for family of four and camping equip.?
Allegro, Marina Estate, Maxi

Pick up after what time? After 4 o'clock Friday

Return by when? By 10 o'clock Monday morning

COST

Basic £29.25 for how many miles? 300 miles

Per extra mile? 5½p

Deposit? not mentioned

Extra for two drivers? £2.50

Prices with/without V.A.T.? Plus V.A.T. at 15%

Insurance included? Included

Reading and writing

What to do if involved in a road accident
Keep cool and concentrate on the essentials:
   Get help for anyone who is injured.
   Call the police if the accident is serious.
   Collect as much information as possible
for your insurance claim.

Informing the police
Not every accident need be reported to the
police, but there are certain circumstances
where you must stop at the scene of the
accident:
  1 If anyone, apart from yourself, has
been injured.
  2 If any vehicle, apart from your own, has
been damaged.
  3 If certain animals have been injured or
killed.
  4 If there is damage to any property on or
near the road.
  The motorist must give his name, address
and registration number (and the owner's
name and address if he is not the owner) to
anyone who has reasonable grounds for
wanting them.
  When someone has been injured the
motorist must also produce his insurance
certificate.
  Only when names and addresses are not
exchanged after such an accident must the
motorist report it to the police—within 24
hours.

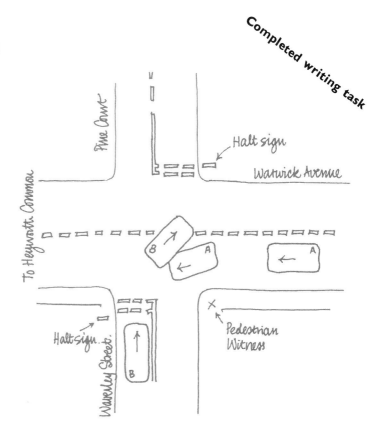

Write a report of the accident as seen from the
position of the pedestrian witness.

At 9.30 on 1 May I was standing
at the corner of Warwick Avenue
and Waverley Street. Car A was
travelling at about 30 m.p.h.
towards Heyworth Common.
Car B was travelling along
Waverley Street and turned right
into Warwick Avenue without
stopping. Car A hit the rear end
of Car B.

Age How it affects the accident rate

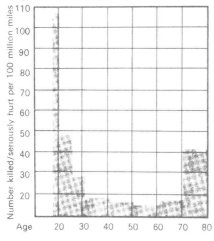

59

13 Finding out who's who

Objectives

1 To give students practice in identifying people by listening to them being described.
2 To give students practice in reading and writing informal party invitations and in identifying houses from a written description.

Tape

Tapescript

Liz: Hello.
Helen: Hi.
Liz: Glad you could make it. Oh you got a drink, great.
Helen: Yes, yes.
Liz: How are you feeling about starting?
Helen: Oh a bit nervous, I don't know. It's always the same really first job, isn't it.
Liz: Oh you shouldn't be. They're a nice lot. Look there's quite a lot of them over there. You can (Yes)...erm...you'll have to get to meet them.
Helen: Yes. Who are they all?
Liz: Well they're mostly students though there's one teacher.
Helen: Yes? Which one's that?
Liz: Can you see...erm... the blonde chap standing next to the tree there...erm... with a sort of white sweater with stripes on it.
Helen: Oh yes.
Liz: He's the sports...
Helen: Grinning all over his face.
Liz: That's right, he's always like that (Yes). Yes, he's a very jolly character. He runs all the sports and he knows all the girls. He's great fun.
Helen: Yes? (Mm) What about the girl next to him? The one next to him. The one all in white. She looks rather glamorous.
Liz: Oh she is... she's ... That's Katy. (Yes). ..erm... she's been doing photography with me. She's quite good really.
Helen: She's going to do pottery?
Liz: ...bit disorganised really. Yes, she will. (Yes) Yes, she'd like to do that.
Helen: Oh that's nice. She looks nice.
Liz: Yes, she's OK. Then there's her sister next to her. The one drinking out of the coke can there. (Yes) She looks a bit funny at the moment but she's OK. She's ...erm... quite good really I should think. The one in the striped thing.

Helen: Yes. And she's going to do pottery as well you reckon. (Huh-huh) Good (Yes). Well that's nice. So what was the one. Katy and...

Liz: Katy and Ann. They're sisters.

Helen: Sisters, fine. OK. Right. Good.

Liz: Yes...erm... there's a nice chap over the other side on the right, wearing a light-coloured sweater and dark trousers. Dark... dark-haired fellow. He's called Jo. (Yes) Well he's really Giovanni. He's Italian but everybody calls him Jo. (Mm) He's a lot of fun. He's a bit slapdash but...erm... he's done photography and you never quite know whether he's coming or going but he's all right really, he's quite nice, very jolly.

Helen: What about the girl next to him with the long... long hair.

Liz: Oh she's OK, yes. She's quite good. I think she's probably doing pottery too. (Yes) She was a photography student.

Helen: What's her name?

Liz: ...erm... oh gosh. I'm so bad at names. Mary, Mary. That's right (OK) yes, yes and...

Helen: So there are two Marys, aren't there? I shall have trouble with that to begin with.

Liz: Are there?

Helen: Yes. Didn't you say that...that one of the sisters was called Mary?

Liz: No. They are Katy and Ann.

Helen: Oh. Right.

Liz: The one in the striped thing is Ann (Right) and the one in white's Katy. And then the big tall chap next to the tree... you can just see him there, dark curly hair (Mm-mm) ...erm... looking at us with the moustache. (Yes) That's Greg. He's very nice. He'll be very friendly. I think... I'm pretty sure he's doing pottery too.

Helen: Good.

Liz: He's a nice chap.

Helen: Well they seem... they seem nice, don't they?

Liz: Why don't you come over and meet them. I'll introduce you to them.

Helen: Well...

Liz: Come on. Be brave.

Helen: All right. I suppose I've got to meet them sometime.

Liz: Yes you have. Come on.

Helen: OK.

Length: 2 min. 37 sec.

Number of speakers: 2.

Setting: An informal college party where a teacher is identifying various guests for a colleague.

Key language

Function: Describing people.

Lexis:
blonde	light-coloured
chap	dark
sweater	dark-haired
stripes	curly
grinning	moustache

Structures: standing next to...
(the girl) with (long hair)
the one...
That's...
she looks...
there's a...chap standing...
over the other side
on the right
wearing...

TEACHING HINTS

Find or draw pictures of people to use as visual aids. Pictures of famous people are motivating; in any case, give every person a name. Teach any unknown lexis or structures in conjunction while describing each picture and then asking the students to look at all the pictures and identify, for example, Jimmy Carter. Students can then describe someone in the class without naming them and the students listening can guess who is being described.

Tasks

Before listening

Ask students if they like meeting new people and how they feel when they go to a party where they know very few people. Ask them what kind of party they like and how often they go to one. Then tell them to open their books at page 26 and to say whether the people in the picture look nice, what they might do for a job or study and who they would choose to go and talk to. Tell them they are going to hear a conversation between two people at the party (but not in the picture): Liz is identifying some people for Helen, who has just arrived and doesn't know anyone.

Listening task

Tell students that their task is to put people's names in the boxes provided. Check students' answers by asking, for example, which one is Katy and accept such answers as 'She's standing next to the teacher. She's got long dark hair and is wearing a white sweater and trousers.' To finish the session, ask students to describe the people not yet identified.

Reading task

Ask students how they invite friends to a party. They may say they do it at school or by telephone. If so, ask them how else you can invite people and so elicit that you can do it by post. Then tell them to open their books at page 27. If you wish, you can focus on the photos of houses at this point. Ask students at which house they would prefer to go to a party and why. Supply any unknown words as necessary. Then ask them to read the letter again and put a tick by the house where the party is to be held. Check they all have the correct answer. For supplementary practice, students can draw a map of Bumpton showing Tudor Cottage and put on it the time and date of the party.

62

Writing task

Tell the students to imagine that they are having a party and that they want to invite an English friend who speaks very little of their language. They don't want to ring him, as they will then have a difficult conversation, probably in English, so they are going to write to him. Compose the letter orally in class, following the same layout and plan of inviting and giving directions as in the printed letter. Then ask students to write the letter in the space provided either in class or for homework.

13   Finding out who's who

Listening

Write the names of the guests at the party above each one.

Reading and writing

Read the letter and decide in which house the party is being held. Tick the correct house and then write to an English friend, inviting him to a party at your home.

```
                    Tudor Cottage,
                    High Street,
                    Bumpton,
                    Oxon,

                    1 July 1980
Dear Jan,
   We are having a party from 7 p.m.
to midnight on Saturday 27 July in
our new house. We do hope you'll come.
   It's very easy to find. When you
come into the village, look for the
main street and we are the third house
on the left as you go towards the
church. It's a black and white house
with an old, white gate, a thatched
roof and a very untidy hedge. You
can park outside.
   Best wishes,

            David
```

(address)

(date)

Dear (name),

We are having a party from (time) to (time) on (day, date) (place). We do hope you'll come.

It's very easy to find. When you come into the (village/town), look for the (street/road) and we are the (first/second, etc) house on the (left/right) as you go towards the (place). It's a (colour) house with (two things to help your friend find it). You can park (outside, etc).

Best wishes,

(name)

14 Fixing an appointment

Objectives

1 To help students understand and follow a conversation about appointments.
2 To give students practice in reading a variety of appointment cards, invitations, messages, and in noting the details in a diary.

Tape

Tapescript

Principal: Well it looks to me as if we shall have to fit him in somewhere. What does Monday morning look like?

Secretary: Well Monday morning is extremely busy. You've got all the short-list interviews.

Principal: Oh goodness. And how long do they go on for?

Secretary: Well the last one is due at... to come at 10 o'clock and will probably go on through until 10.30.

Principal: And then?

Secretary: Then you've got your Japanese agent and you did tell him you'd probably take him out to lunch.

Principal: Yes, well I can't pass that up...erm... what's Tuesday morning look like?

Secretary: Tuesday morning is also very full. You've got a committee meeting, starts at 9.30 probably won't finish until 12.30.

Principal: Huh-Huh. And lunch?

Secretary: Lunch is with your publisher.

Principal: Oh yes. And I do remember that I've got something in the afternoon...erm...from the examining board, haven't I? I've got...

Secretary: Yes. At 2.30. you're expecting the chief examiner (Oh) regarding the review report.

Principal: Oh yes. And I've got... I've got somebody's parents coming.

Secretary: Yes at 4 o'clock Johan Blun's parents are coming.

Principal: And there... isn't there a meeting, a principal's meeting after... anyway he didn't want to be that late...erm ... well, let's have a look at Monday afternoon. What have we got then?

Secretary: Well the lunch with the Japanese agent is probably likely to last until 2.30. (Mm-Mm) At 2.30 you've got the lawyer regarding the planning permission.

Principal: Oh. I've ...yes ...and?

Secretary: Well at 3.30 there's a tutorial with Maria Rosa...

Principal: Oh well hang on...erm... look what we can do ...you... if you could give the lawyer a ring and ask him if he can fix it, the appointment, for Wednesday and if he can't make Wednesday, later in the week. It's not absolutely vital that I should do it then. And give Maria Rosa a ring also if you can contact her, otherwise you can tell her when she arrives and ...erm... I can give... I can definitely give her ... I've got Wednesday clear, haven't I? So... erm... (Yes) I can give her a tutorial on Wednesday morning (Yes) and that gives us two hours so you could ring the Cultural Council and fix it for then. His name's Mr Dennis I think, isn't it?

Secretary: Yes. So I'll ring him and tell him you're expecting him at 2.30 on Monday afternoon.

Principal: OK then.

Secretary: Fine. Thank you.

Length: 2 min. 20 sec.

Number of speakers: 2.

Setting: In the employer's office trying to fit an appointment into a very full schedule.

Key language

Function: Asking for and giving information about the time and duration of someone's appointments.

Lexis:

busy	contract
full	lunch
late	committee meeting
hang on	publisher
contact	lawyer
clear	planning permission
short list	tutorial
interviews	review report
agent	chief examiner
re	principal

Structures: to fit him in
How long do ... go on for?
due at...
start at ... probably won't finish until...
probably likely to last...
you've got ...
fix an appointment
make an appointment

TEACHING HINTS

Most of the structures express the time appointments begin and finish, and their duration, so they are probably best presented and practised within the context of a simple appointments diary. Draw a page of a diary on the board showing the seven days of the week. Tell students that the diary belongs to someone famous. Ask them to suggest the appointments that might be in this person's diary. Fill in the best of these suggestions on the board. This diary can be used to present and practise some of the structures. Much of the key lexis is written in the diary on page 28 in their books. Ask them to look at it. Items such as 'review report' will be of little use to many students. If this is the case spend a short time explaining their general meaning and be happy with students having a passive understanding of them. If, on the other hand, you are teaching students interested in business they may find this lexis extremely useful and you could spend more time on it.

Tasks

Before listening

Ask students to look at the partially filled in diary on page 28 in their books. Check that they understand such items as 're', 'a.m.', 'p.m.', and what the arrows mean. Give them time to read through the appointments before playing the tape.

   Set the scene by asking the students to try and guess, by looking at the kinds of appointments, who this diary belongs to, e.g. a business man, teacher. Tell them they are going to hear two people trying to fit in another appointment. Ask the students to suggest how this might be done, e.g. cancelling, postponing, shortening.

Listening task

Tell students to listen first for the times of the appointments and to fill in the boxes beside each one. Note: not enough information is given to fill in all the boxes. When students have filled in the times tell them to listen for the alterations which the secretary notes in the diary and to do the same in their books. Let them check their answers with each other then with you.

Reading task

Ask students to read the invitations, telegram, message and reminder on page 29. Tell them to underline unknown words and phrases and to try to find out their meaning either by guessing from the context, by asking each other or you, or by using a good dictionary. Now ask them to ring the essential details in each piece. If your students have not done much note-taking before ring the essential details in the note from Jane together. Then ask them to do the rest and check their answers with their neighbour.

Writing task

Check that all students have only ringed the essential information. Now ask them to transfer this information, in note form, into the appropriate slot in the diary.

Listening

Fill in the times of the appointments. Not all the boxes can be filled in.
Show how the appointments are rearranged to fit in Mr Dennis.

MARCH

26
MON

☐ *a.m. Short-list interviews:*
Miss Harrison, Miss Jones
[10.00] *Miss Peters*

[10.30] *Japanese Agent re contract*
↓
? Lunch - Japanese Agent ?

[2.30] *p.m. ~~Lawyer re planning permission~~*
MR DENNIS

[3.30] ~~*Tutorial - Maria Rosa*~~

☐ *Stuart*

27
TUES

[9.30] *am. Committee Meeting*
[12.30]
↓
Lunch publishers

[2.30] *p.m. Review Report and chief*
examiner

[4.00] *Meet Johan Blun's parents*

☐ *Principal's meeting*
↓

28
WED

Lawyer ?
? Maria Rosa. Tutorial

Reading and writing

Underline the essential details in each message.
Fill in the appointments in the diary.

MON 23

TUES 24 11.00 Coffee. Jane's
4.30 Dental appointment

WED 25 Phone Garage a.m.

THURS 26 10 a.m. Hurn Airport —
Peter

FRI 27

SAT 28 8.00 Smythe's 25th
Wedding Anniversary

SUN 29

POST OFFICE

INLAND TELEGRAM
FOR POSTAGE STAMPS

Charge		Chargeable Words	Sent at/by
Tariff excl RP £			
VAT £			
RP £		Circulation	
TOTAL £			

Prefix	Handed in	Service instructions	Actual Words

BLOCK LETTERS THROUGHOUT PLEASE

To

ARRIVING HURN AIRPORT 10 A.M.
THURSDAY STOP PLEASE MEET ME STOP
LOVE PETER STOP

The particulars on the back of this form should be completed.

Mon. morning
Dropped by but
you are out!
Come over for a
coffee + chat
tomorrow — 11 a.m.
love Jane

Sarah
Garage phoned
— car will be
ready Wed. —
Probably.
— phone Wed.
a.m. to check.
John

DAWSON'S DENTAL SURGERY

Reminder

Your next appointment is

24 May 4.30 p.m.

Mr and Mrs Smythe
request the company of

Mr and Mrs Mead

on the occasion of their
25th Wedding Anniversary
on Saturday 28 May at 8 p.m.

R.S.V.P. THE MANOR HOUSE, BURFORD ON AVON, HAMPSHIRE

15 Making enquiries at a travel agency

Objectives

1 To give students practice in sifting out specific travel information from a conversation between a travel agent and customer.
2 To give students practice in reading simple rules about the countryside and in writing signs to implement these rules.

Tape

Tapescript

Travel agent: Good morning Madam. Can I help you?

Customer: Ah yes. I hope so. I've got a bit of a problem actually. I want to go to ...er... Edinburgh for the Festival (Oh yes) and I'm not too sure of the best way to get there (Mm-mm) I've got a car but it's ...er... not in very good condition and I was just wondering first of all if you could tell me how long you think it'd take me to drive up there.

Travel agent: Well if you go up the motorway I suppose about eight hours.

Customer: Eight hours!

Travel agent: Mm it's a long way.

Customer: Yes it is a long way and I suppose petrol prices the way they are at the moment it'd be a bit expensive too.

Travel agent: Well, well yes. It'd probably cost you about £10, (Mm) depends on your car.

Customer: Yes the car's the trouble. I don't know what kind of condition I'd arrive in. Tell me ... Now what about ...erm...coach? (Yes) Because I've been told that's fairly reasonable.

Travel agent: Oh it is. It's very good. It costs about £14 in fact London to Edinburgh.

Customer: Mm. That's not too bad.

Travel agent: Very reasonable.

Customer: On the other hand it takes quite a long time.

Travel agent: Yes it takes about ten hours.

Customer: Ten hours!

Travel agent: Well yes but you can go at night so you might get some sleep anyway.

Customer: Oh no! I never sleep sitting up.

Travel agent: No? Well...

Customer: Don't think so. What about the train then?

71

Travel agent: Yes...erm... let me see. It takes five hours in fact from London to Edinburgh ...erm... and it costs £21 single.

Customer: £21 single.

Travel agent: Mm. Well it's a lot of money but of course you can then sleep at night and so on.

Customer: Yes, you'd arrive in ... feeling OK I suppose.

Travel agent: Mm. Yes.

Customer: What I'd really like to do of course is go the whole hog and go by plane. Can you tell me about that?

Travel agent: Mm-mm. Yes, of course...erm... the London to Edinburgh single... let me see... £38 but of course it only takes just over an hour. It takes seventy minutes.

Customer: Really?

Travel agent: Yes (Ah.) You're there in no time.

Customer: Wonderful. That'd be a wonderful start to the holiday.

Travel agent: Mm. Shall I book you a ticket?

Customer: Well, look I tell you what. I really ought to think about it. Thanks so much for your help but I think I'll... I'll come back to you if that's OK.

Travel agent: Mm-mm.

Length: 2 min. 5 sec.
Number of speakers: 2.
Setting: A travel agency.

Key language

Function: Asking for and giving basic travel information.

Lexis:
drive	reasonable
motorway	take (time)
cost	single
coach	travel agent

Structures: I want to ...
How long...?
What about...?
Can you tell me about...?
If you... I suppose ...
It'd probably cost you...
It takes...
It costs...

TEACHING HINTS

To present and practise the lexical and structural items new to the students or in need of revision, use the context of a class trip to London, for example. First present and practise the questions the students would need to ask in order to decide how to travel there. Then act the part of a travel agent and give them the answers to their questions.

Tasks

Before listening

Locate Edinburgh and London on a map of Great Britain. Find out if anyone has been to either city or has made the journey between them. If possible, show some pictures of both cities to bring them to life in the students' minds and present the Edinburgh Festival. (This is held every September and is a very good festival of music, theatre and Scottish culture.) Then set the scene by presenting the characters (a travel agent and a woman who wants to go to the Edinburgh Festival), the setting (a London travel agency) and ask them if it's a long or a short journey and how they would make the journey to acquaint them with the woman's problem.

Listening task

Tell students to listen first in order to find out how long the journeys take. Ask them to complete the number of hours under each picture. Then ask them to listen again for the cost of travelling and to fill in the section at the bottom. Play the tape as many times as necessary. Let them check their answers with each other and then with you. Round off the session by asking them which way they think the woman should go to Edinburgh.

Reading task

Enthuse students about the beauty of the Scottish countryside. If possible show them a picture of the Highlands or of a Loch. Then introduce the problem of litter and the damage tourists do. Present any new vocabulary at this point. Get students thinking about all the things people do wrong in the countryside and how they could stop them. Then ask them to look at page 31 in their books, read the *Country Code* to themselves and put the appropriate number in the corner of each picture. Let them check their answers with each other and with you.

Writing task

Now ask students to think up short notices to put in the boxes provided under each picture. Suggest they phrase them 'No...(-ing...)', 'Do not...', or 'Please...'. Write at least one sign with the whole class. For example, take picture A and elicit ideas from the class, supplying vocabulary if needed. Phrase their ideas correctly and let everybody practise, e.g. 'No dogs', 'Do not let your dog off lead', 'Please control your dog'. Then let the class choose the best sign and write it in their books. When you feel the students are prepared, let them think about each of the remaining signs and ask you for any words they need. They can then write the signs in class, for homework or ideally, partly in class and partly for homework. In the latter case, walk around the class while the students are writing, so that you can help or correct any student before they have got very far with the task. As a possible follow-up, ask the class to design full-size posters based on the signs to pin up in the classroom or at home.

Listening

Fill in the missing information.

Scotland

Newcastle to Edinburgh $2\frac{1}{2}$ hours
London to Edinburgh   **8** hours
Manchester to Glasgow   4 hours
Bristol to Glasgow   7 hours

Newcastle to Edinburgh $4\frac{1}{2}$ hours
London to Edinburgh   **10** hours
Manchester to Glasgow $8\frac{1}{2}$ hours

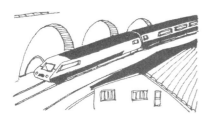

Newcastle to Edinburgh 2 hours
London to Edinburgh   **5** hours
Manchester to Glasgow   4 hours
Bristol to Glasgow $6\frac{1}{2}$ hours

London to Aberdeen   80 mins
London to Edinburgh   **70** mins
London to Glasgow   70 mins
London to Inverness   120 mins

Travel to Scotland is not expensive:
From London to Edinburgh by car £ **10**
                        by coach £ **14**
                        by train £ **21**
                        by plane £ **38**

Reading and writing

When in Scotland tourists often forget to follow the *Country Code* below. Read the list of things you should and shouldn't do and write the appropriate number in each picture. Then write a sign underneath each one to stop people from doing things wrong.

THE COUNTRY CODE

1 Guard against fire
2 Fasten all gates
3 Keep dogs under control
4 Keep to paths across farmland
5 Avoid damaging fences, hedges, walls

6 Leave no litter
7 Safeguard water supplies
8 Protect wild life, wild plants and trees
9 Go carefully on country roads

No. 3 — Keep your dog on a lead.	No. 8 — Protect wild life.	No. 1 — Danger! No smoking or campfires.
No. 9 — Drive with care.	No. 6 — Take your litter with you.	No. 2 — Please shut the gate.
No. 5 — Respect the countryside.	No. 4 — Keep to the path.	No. 7 — Fresh drinking water. Do not pollute.

75   *Note*: These are just some of the many possible correct answers. Encourage your students to be as inventive and original as their grasp of English will allow.

16 Shopping

Objectives

1 To help students understand and follow simple street directions.
2 To give students practice in reading the prices of basic food products as they appear in advertisements and in calculating their total cost and then in compiling a shopping list.

Tape

Tapescript

Fiona: OK Judy. I've got the list here. Erm... now, d'you think there's anything else you need?

Judy: No, that's everything actually. You don't mind going, Fiona, do you?

Fiona: No! I like shopping, and anyway, I'd like to find my way around here a little bit.

Judy: Oh, that's tremendous then. Well, shall we just run through the shopping list to make sure you know where all the shops are?

Fiona: Good idea. Fine. OK, here goes. Er, the first thing I've got is one large white loaf. Now, where shall I get that from?

Judy: Yes, if you get that from the baker's...(From the baker's) so that it's nice and fresh.

Fiona: Yes, OK, erm...how do I get there from here?

Judy: Well, it's not very far. You just go down New Street, which is where we are, (Yes) and it's on the other side of the road on the corner of High Street and New Street, so it's on the left.

Fiona: Good. Fine. Got that... and er...a pound of apples. Now, where d'you usually buy your apples?

Judy: At the greengrocer's (Uh-huh) you know the one. It's very very close. It's next to the baker's...actually before you get to the baker's.

Fiona: On the left-hand side of New Street?

Judy: Right. It's on the same side of the road as the baker's.

Fiona: OK, erm...a pound of cheese.

Judy: Yes, you get that from the Co-op, where there's plenty of choice.

Fiona: From the Co-op. (Yes) Mm-mm.

Judy: And again that's quite easy to get to. (Mm) You go right the way down New Street until you get to the High Street.

Fiona: Oh, so it's opposite.

Judy: That's right, and (Uh-huh) the Co-op is on the other side of the road just opposite New Street and you can't miss it.

Fiona: Yes. OK. So, that's er...cheese at the Co-op, er... box of tissues. Now, where would you like me to get those from?

Judy: Probably the chemist is best, (The chemist, mm) I should think. It's usually cheaper there. (OK) And that's on this side of the road, so you just go down New Street and it's on the right. It's on... again on the corner of High Street and New Street, just opposite the baker's.

Fiona: Oh yes. Yes, I remember. Yes. Fine. Erm...and a large tube of toothpaste. Er...shall I get that from the chemist as well?

Judy: Probably best to, yes. It'll save you time too.

Fiona: OK. Fine. And er...oh, the...yes, the local newspaper.

Judy: Yes, get that from the newsagent's.

Fiona: Yes, right.

Judy: Now, that is in the High Street (Yes) on the opposite corner to the Co-op. There's a very small street in between.

Fiona: Oh, I think I've seen it. (Yes) Yes, it's actually on the corner.

Judy: It's on the corner opposite the Co-op – quite a small shop.

Fiona: Fine. And last of all airmail letter...an airmail letter.

Judy: Ah, yes. Now if you get that from the Post Office (Mm-mm) which is next to the Co-op the other side. There's the...

Fiona: Next to the Co-op...

Judy: Yes, so it's on High Street (Yes) and it's...there's the Post Office, then the Co-op, and then over the road are the newsagents. So there's those three shops in the High Street.

Fiona: Right then. Well, I'll be off now.

Judy: That's lovely. Thanks very much.

Fiona: OK. See you in half an hour or so.

Judy: OK. See you later.

Fiona: Bye.

Judy: Bye.

Length: 2 min. 52 sec.
Number of speakers: 2.
Setting: A visiting friend has offered to do the shopping and before leaving she enquires where to buy the individual items on the shopping list.

Key language

Function: Asking for and giving directions.

Lexis:
list	newsagent
large white loaf	post office
a pound of apples	next to
cheese	opposite
a box of tissues	in between
large tube of toothpaste	on the other side (of...)
local newspaper	on the same side (as...)
airmail letter	on this side
baker	on the left/right (-hand side)
greengrocer	on the corner
Co-op	go (right the way) down
chemist	until you get to

before you get to   it's very close
it's easy   you can't miss it
it's not very far

Structures: You (just) go down... and it's...
                You get...from the ...

TEACHING HINTS

Realia or visual aids would probably be the best way to teach the items on the
shopping list and the names of shops. You may need to explain that the Co-op
(short for Co-operative Wholesale Society Ltd) is a supermarket, and that Co-ops
are to be found throughout Britain. You will also have to explain the
abbreviations used on page 32 in the Student's Book and perhaps teach one or
two more commonly occurring ones, e.g. doz.=dozen, oz.=ounce. This will lead
you on to talking about metric equivalents, e.g. 1kg = 2.2 lb approximately. At
the moment weights, volume and length are usually printed on products in both
the metric and the British systems (see page 33 in Student's Book).

The lexis describing the position of things can be introduced and practised by
talking about the positions of people and objects in the classroom. This could
easily be developed into a simple game:

Student A: The person/thing I'm thinking of is sitting on the other side of the
                room.

The other students try to find out who/what by asking questions about his/its
position:

Student B: Is he/it sitting next to Paul?

You can introduce and practise giving simple directions by drawing a road on the
board and giving it the name of the local main street. Then ask students to tell
you what shops and other buildings there are along it. Make a list of these and
then ask students to say where the shops are relative to one another. As they do
this mark the positions on the road. This can then be used to drill:

Where's the ...?
You go down the main street and it's ... You can't miss it.

When students are fairly confident manipulating these structures they can have
further practice in pairs. Each member of a pair draws a very simple map, only
one or two streets, and marks the positions of the baker, greengrocer, newsagent,
supermarket, chemist, and post office. It is important he keeps this hidden from
his partner. His partner then asks him for directions to these shops and marks
their position according to the directions received. At the end of the exercise they
can look at each other's maps to see if they match.

Tasks

Before listening

If the previous exercises have been done the students will be fairly well prepared
to listen to the tape. Tell them that the conversation takes place in Judy's house,
marked on the map on page 32 in the Student's Book.

Listening task

Before playing the tape for the first time tell the students to listen for and try to jot down the shops where the items are to be bought. When this has been successfully completed ask them to listen to the directions given and to label the shops on the map. Let them check their answers with each other and with you.

Reading task

Students should begin by looking at the advertisements and try to match them to the items on the list and in this way they will probably be able to deduce the meanings of the abbreviations and vocabulary. The task then is simply to calculate the total cost of the shopping on the list. This might also be a good opportunity to revise numbers.

Writing task

Ask students to make up their own shopping lists from the advertisement. In pairs, they should then work out the cost of each other's shopping.

16 Shopping

Listening

Make a list of the shops where the items are to be bought.
Label the positions of these shops on the map.

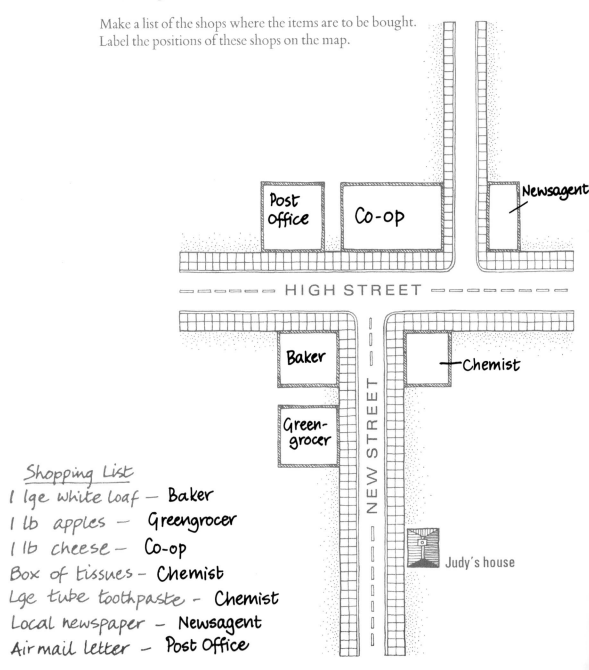

Post
Office

Co-op

Newsagent

HIGH STREET

Baker

Chemist

Green-
grocer

NEW STREET

Judy's house

Shopping List
1 lge white loaf — Baker
1 lb apples — Greengrocer
1 lb cheese — Co-op
Box of tissues — Chemist
Lge tube toothpaste — Chemist
Local newspaper — Newsagent
Airmail letter — Post Office

Reading and writing

How much will this shopping cost?

1½ kg flour	33p
1 pkt tea	19½p
1 litre oil	79p
2 pkts biscuits	64p
2 cans coke	27p
250g butter	36p
1lb jam	29½p
100g coffee	99p
	£3.87

Now make up your own shopping list of these things and ask a neighbour to work out how much your shopping will cost.

81

17 Moving in

Objectives

1 To give students practice in listening to two people deciding where to put items of furniture and then in marking these positions on a plan of the room.
2 To give students practice in buying by post, i.e. reading a catalogue and filling in an order form.

Tape

Tapescript

Rod: Mm, it's not a bad size room, is it?

Liz: Oh, it's great! Oh, and look at that fireplace! Oh, we can have the two chairs right in front of the fireplace there in the middle of the room and toast our feet.

Rod: The first thing we ought to do is just decide where the bed's going.

Liz: Oh, well... (So) what about right here next to the door (Yes) sort of behind the door as you come in?

Rod: Yes, that's a good idea – just as you come in, just in that corner there.

Liz: Yes. Well now, let's think. What else?

Rod: What else is there? Erm...well there's that huge wardrobe of yours...(Mm) that's got to go somewhere.

Liz: What about over here – y'know – across from the fireplace there, because then, in that little corner where it...where the wall goes back...look, over there. (Mm) That'd do, wouldn't it?

Rod: OK, well we'll put the wardrobe there then. (Yes) OK? So the wardrobe's opposite the fireplace.

Liz: Er...(OK) what about your desk? (Er) Where are you going to put that?

Rod: Er...I need lots of light, so I think in that far corner in between the two windows, OK?

Liz: Oh, I see in the corner there (Yes) yes. (Erm) Yes, that'd be good.

Rod: So the desk goes there.

Liz: So you'd have your chair with your back to the fireplace? (Yes) Yes, that'll be all right.

Rod: Yes. And there's (Yes) the chest of drawers.

Liz: Oh, that'd be nice in between the two windows there, right in the middle. (Yes) It really...come on, I know you're going to like it. (OK) Come on, let's shove it over there. (I mean) I bet...I er...

Rod: I knew you'd ask me to move it.

Liz: Come on. Let's go.

Rod: OK. Let's go then. All right.

Liz: Nearly there! That's got it.

Rod: God, what on earth have you got in there?

Liz: Well, there's nothing much in there. I emptied it... most of it out.

Rod: Oh God, my back hurts!

Liz: There! Wait a minute. Let me stand back and have a look.

Rod: Yes, it's not bad...sticks out a bit.

Liz: No, it's fine. (OK) What about the TV? Where are we going to put that?

Rod: Er...it's really got to go in the opposite corner, hasn't it? (Mm) Opposite the desk, that is.

Liz: Oh, you mean in the corner between the windows and the fireplace? (Yes) Yes.

Rod: And then the stereo, er... the amplifier underneath the television and then the two speakers one on either side of the fireplace.

Liz: Yes, that'd be good. (Erm) Well lovely! So it'll all fit in beautifully! (Yes) What else...what else have we got?

Rod: It's the er...there's the bookcase, isn't there? Erm...

Liz: Oh Lord...where'll we put that?

Rod: Well, as you come in the door, er...immediately on the er... left-hand side...

Liz: Oh along that wall there you mean?

Rod: because that's...there's just about enough space there. There's about two feet, so it shouldn't stick out too much, no.

Liz: Yes, it's not very wide is it? So you come in the door (Yes) and then the bookcase is right there on the left. (Yes) There's a long way from your desk, though.

Rod: Well, exercise'll do me good, won't it? Er...table lamp. Well, we can just put that er...

Liz: On the chest of drawers. (Yes) When it's...(Mm) Yes. That'd be nice.

Rod: And no matter who wants to use it, you know.

Liz: Yes. Oh this is going to be lovely. When are we going to get it all in? Now?

Rod: Er...no, not now. Let's just go to the kitchen and er... sort that out and have a cup of tea, eh.

Liz: Oh, ha-ha, good. (Right) Yes, I haven't seen the kitchen. Come on.

Rod: Come on then. Let's go.

Length: 2 min. 42 sec.

Number of speakers: 2.

Setting: A bare room in a small flat recently rented by the speakers.

Key language

Function: Suggesting and agreeing locations for items of furniture.

Lexis: fireplace
in that corner
wardrobe
the wall goes back
desk
window
chest of drawers
stereo (= record player)

amplifier
bookcase
on the left-hand side
table lamp

83

Structures: in the middle of...
next to...
behind...
across from...
opposite...
between...
underneath...
We can have ...
What about...
We'll put...
So...goes...
That'd be nice...
It's got to go...

TEACHING HINTS

Use the sketches on page 34 in the Student's Book or magazine pictures to teach
the names of the items of furniture. Then draw a plan of a room on the
blackboard and present the prepositions of place by sketching in furniture and
describing its location both in the room and in relation to the other items of
furniture in the room. Give students practice in this and in locating their
classroom furniture. The structural exponents of suggesting are less crucial to an
understanding of the extract on tape, but if you wish to teach or revise some or all
of them, tell the students to re-design their classroom. Make some suggestions
yourself first, to present the structure of your choice, and then ask the students to
use the same pattern when making their suggestions. For further practice, ask the
students to re-design an area of the town the school is in.

Tasks

Before listening

Arouse students' interest in moving into a new home by asking them what kind of
house/flat/room they would choose, what furniture they would buy, where they
would like the house to be, etc. Then set the scene for the tape by introducing the
characters Rod and Liz (using suitable visual aids of a young husband and wife if
possible). Tell them they are going to hear Rod and Liz discuss where to put
items of furniture in their new home.

Listening task

Tell students that their task is to sketch the furniture as shown in exactly the right
place on the plan of the room. When the majority of the students have finished
the task, let them compare and check their answers. Finally, draw a copy of the
room plan on the board and get the class to tell you exactly where to sketch in the
furniture. In this way you can check that everyone has completed the task
successfully.

Reading task

Present the idea of buying things by post and teach 'catalogue' if you wish. Set the scene by telling students they are going to buy three new things for Rod and Liz's new home. Ask students to read the extracts describing the items in the picture. Tell them to identify or check they understand what each item is by finding the numbered item in the picture. Check they have done this by asking, for example, how much number 7 costs and which number in the picture is on the pillow.

Writing task

Now ask the students, either individually or as a class, to select three items they would like to buy for the flat. Check they understand all the headings on the order form and then ask them to fill in the form either in class or for homework.

Listening

Draw the pieces of furniture in the right places in the room.

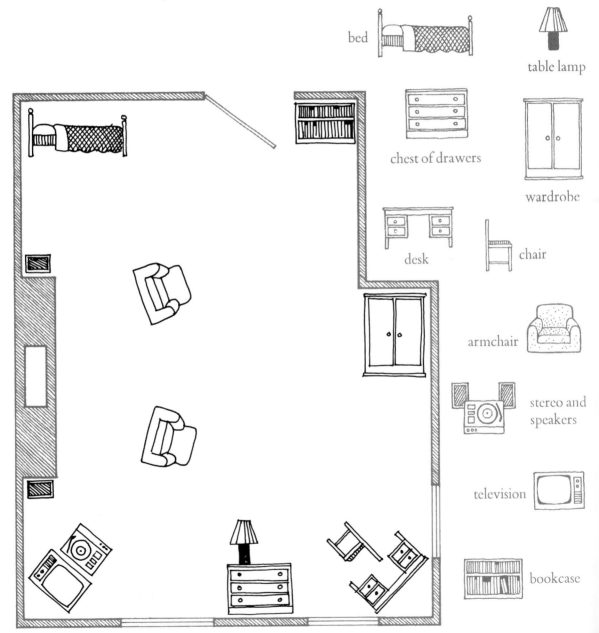

bed

table lamp

chest of drawers

wardrobe

desk

chair

armchair

stereo and speakers

television

bookcase

Reading and writing

Choose three items not mentioned on the tape and order them for Rod Smith's new flat. The address of the flat is 6 Norton Gardens, Brighton. The telephone number is 859067. Make out the order using the name Rod Smith.

1/**Bedside table.** White plastic. 40 × 40 × 40cm. 5846 **£5.65**

2/**Round mirror.** A simple mirror with a coloured plastic frame 24cm diameter. Available in white, yellow, red and brown. 3650 **£1.25**

3/**Duvets.** The best and the cheapest to be found. Machine washable.
Single: 135 × 200cm 8053 **£13.50**
Double: 200 × 200cm 8061 **£15.50**

4/**Pillow.** 45 × 68cm 8088 **£4.00**

5/**Towels.** Thick white cotton towelling with a wide blue stripe.
Hand towel: 55 × 100cm 9122 **£1.10**
Bath towel: 75 × 135cm 9130 **£2.25**

6/**Bed.** The most important single item of furniture you may ever buy. Ours is wood-framed, interior sprung and covered in a choice of really nice blue or brown cotton.
Single: 5853 **£47.00**
Double: 5854 **£63.00**
Large double: 5855 **£89.00**

7/**Rugs.** Handwoven cotton yarn rugs from India. 1378 **£15.95**

8/**Linens.** White sheets, pillowcases and duvet covers.
Single sheet: 1890 **£6.50**
Double sheet: 1871 **£7.50**
Large double sheet: 1892 **£10.50**
Pillowcases: 1900 **£3.45** a pair
Single duvet cover: 3490 **£12.50**
Double duvet cover: 3491 **£15.50**

9/**Blanket.** Thick and cuddly blanket in 100% acrylic fibre which makes it hardwearing and machine washable. Available in blue or brown.

Single: 178 × 230cm 9858 **£5.95**
Double: 230 × 255cm 9866 **£8.25**

10/**Wardrobe.** Plenty of hanging space. 201 × 105 × 56cm 5890 **£75.75**

11/**Dressing table.** The mirror is sold as a separate item.
Dressing table: 67 × 76 × 46cm 5898 **£39.00**
Mirror: 5897 **£17.50**

12/**Three drawer chest.** 67 × 76 × 46cm 5893 **£39.00**

Please complete all details in BLOCK CAPITALS and send this order to: Home Designs Ltd, P.O. Box 20, Western Road, Wellington, Somerset, WW8 1PA. Telephone Wellington (082 347) 76441

Initials	R	Surname	SMITH	Delivery address if different from that shown on left		
Address	6 NORTON GARDENS			Initials		Surname
	BRIGHTON			Address		
Postcode				Postcode		
Telephone nos. work/daytime				Telephone nos. work/daytime		
Telephone nos. Home	BRIGHTON 859067			Telephone nos. Home		

Special delivery instructions (e.g. leave in garage):

Office use only	Item description	Item Code No. (if no Code shown item not available by mail)	Colour	2nd choice colour	Qnty.	Item cash price	Total cash price	Office use only
	BEDSIDE TABLE	F 5846	WHITE	—	1	£5.65	£5.65	
	DUVET	F 8061	—	—	1	£15.50	£15.50	
	DRESSING TABLE	F 5898	—	—	1	£39.00	£39.00	
							£60.15	

18 Phoning a garage

Objectives

1 To help students understand and follow a conversation about the condition of a car.
2 To give students practice in (a) reading short reports about car performance; (b) sifting this information to make choices according to certain criteria; and (c) choosing the car they most prefer and stating reasons for the choice.

Tape

Tapescript

Mechanic: Hello. Workshop.
Mrs Perry: Oh. Hello. This is Mrs Perry. I brought in an Austin 1300 last week for its MOT. I was just wondering how it'd got on.
Mechanic: Oh Mrs Perry. I'm sorry...erm... it failed really badly...erm... you've got lots of problems there I'm afraid.
Mrs Perry: That's terrible.
Mechanic: Oh dear. There's all sorts of things...erm...
Mrs Perry: Well, what's the matter with it?
Mechanic: Well, the exhaust system's in a real mess...erm...
Mrs Perry: The exhaust? That's...that's...that sort of tube that goes underneath there.
Mechanic: That's right. Yes, you know, takes the gases away from the engine. Well look there's an enormous hole in the silencer.
Mrs Perry: A hole?
Mechanic: Yes. I'm just going to have to...
Mrs Perry: I wonder if that's why it's been making rather a noise.
Mechanic: Well, it might have something to do with it. You know it just needs completely replacing the whole exhaust system.
Mrs Perry: Oh dear.
Mechanic: ...erm... then...then... then there's your headlights...
Mrs Perry: Headlights?
Mechanic: Yes Mrs Perry your headlights. The ...er ... you know, the things that shine out at the front of the car.
Mrs Perry: Oh I know what they are but what's the matter with them?
Mechanic: Well it does help if they shine out in a ... straight. They...erm... they're way off alignment and we're going to...we're just going to have to check them very carefully and re-set them.
Mrs Perry: Well at least that isn't a big job is it.

Mechanic: Well maybe not but then there's the radiator.

Mrs Perry: What? There's nothing the matter with the radiator.

Mechanic: I'm afraid so. The radiator's just not working properly. There's water all over the place...erm...

Mrs Perry: Dear, dear.

Mechanic: It seems to be leaking like a sieve. I can only think we're going to have to replace the whole radiator.

Mrs Perry: Oh goodness. How much is all that going to cost?

Mechanic: Oh. I couldn't even hazard a guess at this stage...erm...

Mrs Perry: Oh come on. Give me an idea. About £100?

Mechanic: Well you know, one thing and another I...I mean you might get away with £100 yes. Let's talk about £100 to be on the safe side.

Mrs Perry: Oh. All right. When shall I come in?

Mechanic: Well give us a ring tomorrow morning.

Mrs Perry: OK. I will. Bye.

Mechanic: Bye.

Length: 2 min. 7 sec.

Number of speakers: 2.

Setting: Car owner phones the garage to find out the condition of her car.

Key language

Function: Saying what is wrong with a car and saying what will have to be done.

Lexis:

MOT	check
exhaust system	matter with
headlights	leaking
radiator	all over the place
silencer	to be on the safe side
real mess	might get away with
replace	failed
shine	not working properly
way off alignment	enormous
straight	hole
re-set	

Structures: ...needs doing

we are (just) going to have to ...

... not working properly

... in a real mess

TEACHING HINTS

Either draw or find a picture of a dilapidated house with a couple of prospective buyers. Use this to practise saying what is wrong with the house. You can use the same aid to practise saying what will have to be done to it. You could build up a dialogue between the couple, getting the students to suggest the kind of thing they might be saying to each other.

The lexis specific to cars would best be introduced and practised using the diagram of a car on page 36 in the Student's Book. The diagram makes much of this lexis clear.

Tasks

Before listening

Set the scene by explaining what an MOT test is. (Each year in Britain, cars which are over three years old have to pass a test of road-worthiness and general safety. The test checks lighting equipment, steering and suspension, brakes, tyres and wheels, seat belts, windscreen washers and wipers, horn, exhaust system and body work. MOT stands for the Ministry of Transport.) Students who are interested in cars may want to know the names of more parts. These students could use the diagram and label more of the parts shown. Ask students to say what kind of thing could go wrong with the parts of the car labelled and feed in more of the key lexis as needed. Tell students they are going to hear a woman phone the garage to find out about her car.

Listening task

Tell students to listen first for the parts of the car which are faulty. Tell them that if the part is not mentioned then it is all right and they should put a tick on the grid in the 'OK' column. Tell them that you are going to play the tape again and that this time they have to listen for the details given about the fault. They should record this information on the grid under 'Notes'. Finally they have to listen for how much the mechanic estimates the repairs will cost and to tick the appropriate amount under the grid. Let them check their answers together and with you.

Reading task

Ask students to read the information about each of the cars and to underline items needing explanation. Encourage students to deduce the meaning of unknown items from their context. For example, a student who underlines 'economical' might be expected to deduce its meaning by looking at the way it is used in the description of the Fiat 126 'Economical 47 mpg'. On the other hand explanations of '2-star' may have to be supplied.

Writing task

Let students discuss in small groups or pairs which car would best suit Mrs Bennett and which Mr Bennett. Ask each group to jot down reasons for the choice, then ask one person from each group to tell the rest of the class his group's choice and their reasons. Some groups may want to change their minds before writing their answers. Students who are interested in cars will probably enjoy the final writing task and may want to choose a car which is not shown. This does not matter, of course.

18   Phoning a garage

Listening

Fill in the information about the car on the grid.

1 gear lever on gearbox
2 exhaust system (and silencer)
3 radiator (cools the water which circulates through the engine)
4 petrol tank
5 petrol filler
6 headlights

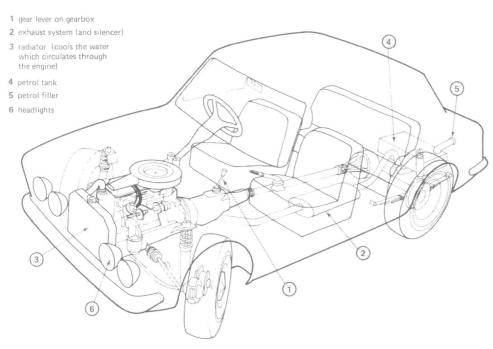

PART OF CAR	O.K.	NEEDS ATTENTION	NOTES
1	✓		
2		✓	Enormous hole in silencer — replace
3		✓	Leaking — replace
4	✓		
5	✓		
6		✓	not straight - reset

How much will the repairs cost?
– less than £100? ✓
– exactly £100?
– more than £100?

Tick the correct amount.

91

Reading and writing

Which car would best suit the following people? Give reasons.

1 Mrs Bennett, mother of three (aged 7, 9, 11) needs a car for shopping, taking children to school.
2 Mr Bennett drives 40 miles a day to work. He also needs a car for family holidays etc.
3 Which car would you choose for yourself and why?

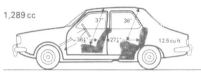

RENAULT 12

1,289 cc

Running costs
Economical – 29 mpg
Verdict
A very likeable medium-sized family saloon. Very comfortable and reliable, with quick acceleration and quiet cruising.

MGB

1,798 cc

Running costs
Petrol: 26 mpg
Verdict
Fast, with good handling and braking. Convertible, one of the few soft top sports cars left.

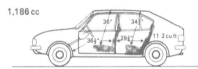

ALFASUD

1,186 cc

Running costs
A little thirsty for 1200 cc – 28 mpg.
Verdict
Great fun to drive, and quite roomy for its size. Fairly reliable, but poor bodywork.

HONDA CIVIC

1,169 cc

Running costs
Quite economical, 35 mpg
Verdict
Lively small car — fun to drive. Fairly comfortable but road noise makes it less good for long, fast drives. Useful luggage carrier with only two people.

SAAB 99

1,985 cc

Running costs
Latest 2-litre manual versions not tested, earlier 1·85 and 2·0 automatic – 27 mpg.
Verdict
Very solid and well-engineered (particularly for safety). Not a sporty car, but a quiet, comfortable touring saloon. Plenty of luggage space. Overall, quite good value new.

FIAT 126

594 cc

Running costs
Economical 47 mpg, 2-star.
Verdict
Very economical, but not very comfortable, not roomy, and very noisy.

Mrs Bennett

Honda Civic. Quite economical, good luggage carrier, lively.

Mr Bennett

Saab 99. Roomy, safe, quite comfortable.

My Choice

I would choose the MGB convertible because it's fast and good fun to drive. I also like cars which don't keep the sun out in summer!

19 Flat hunting

Objectives

1 To give students practice in sifting information from a conversation about housing advertisements and so in inferring someone's housing requirements.
2 To give students practice in reading advertisements in a shop window and then in writing them.

Tape

Tapescript

Helen: Hi.

Rod: Hi.

Helen: Gosh, you're not still looking for a flat are you?

Rod: Yes. I've been looking for six weeks now. It's driving me mad you know.

Helen: Do you want any help?

Rod: Yes you'd be a great help actually.

Helen: Let's have a look at the newspaper together.

Rod: Yes.

Helen: What about that one 'Abingdon Road, single attic bedsitter'...er...

Rod: No single's no good because there's two of us you see.

Helen: Yes? OK. Have you ...Have you... got a limit as to how much you want to spend?

Rod: Yes. It mustn't be more than £30 a week (OK) I think that's about the maximum you know.

Helen: Right. OK. What about the next one then?

Rod: 'Accommodation Kennington' (Yes) 'suit non-smoking person'. That's no good because Liz smokes so...

Helen: Does she?

Rod: Yes.

Helen: I thought she'd stopped.

Rod: Well she tried to give up but you know like everything else she tries it for a couple of days and that's it.

Helen: Yes? Well maybe you could persuade her to give up (Yes) ... still Kennington's not very central is it.

Rod: No and see I haven't got a car and it's much too far to cycle.

Helen: Right.

Rod: ...erm... 'available immediately'. God this sounds good! Look at that!

Helen: 'Exceptionally attractive, well-appointed Cotswold house.' Gosh yes! Oh but look, it's eleven miles from Oxford. (Mm). Yes. That'd be hopeless. How far do you reckon you could cycle, I mean eleven miles?

93

Rod: I reckon about, no, two or three miles is the limit really.
Helen: Yes?
Rod: I'm getting old you know.
Helen: Oh that's out then. Oh but it does look fantastic, doesn't it?
Rod: 'Available soon. Furnished flat. Suitable young couple.'
Helen: Ah. That's nice.
Rod: Ah. Furnished. Must be unfurnished.
Helen: Why?
Rod: She's got all that old stuff of her mother's you know.
Helen: You've got to use that?
Rod: Yes we have really.
Helen: That's no good then.
Rod: So that's out.
Helen: 'Bedsitting room available now for lady.' Well that'd be all right for Liz but not for you.
Rod: No ... that's no good.
Helen: ...erm... 'Prefer someone away on Sunday.' What a funny idea!
Rod: Mm. 'Bedsit £14. Flat £28.' Mm. That's a possibility. What's this 'Room in shared house £25 per week, central.'
Helen: Well it's central... central.
Rod: No good though.
Helen: Why?
Rod: It's just a room you see. We need something self-contained.
Helen: Yes. It could be quite a big one though. Still there are two of you aren't there.
Rod: Yes (Yes) I think that that ...erm... early one is the only possibility really.
Helen: Yes. Well give them a ring see what they say.
Rod: Yes I'm getting sick of this, shall we have a cup of coffee?
Helen: Yes let's finish.

Length: 2 min. 13 sec.
Number of speakers: 2.
Setting: Two friends looking at advertisements for accommodation in the newspaper.

Key language

Function: Selecting and rejecting houses/flats advertised in a newspaper.

Lexis:		
single	furnished	hopeless
double	unfurnished	That's no good
bedsitter	self-contained	That's out
maximum	let	That's a possibility
central	rent	That's the only possibility

Structures: it mustn't be...   this sounds...

it must be...   we need...

TEACHING HINTS

First present and practise the new housing vocabulary with the aid of magazine pictures, estate agents' photographs or blackboard drawings. Then tell the students about a particular person's housing needs and practise the phrases of selection and rejection (e.g. 'That's out') by selecting a house for them. Present the structures listed in the setting of an estate agent's office. The situation is that the particular person mentioned above and/or the students themselves are telling the estate agent about the type of accommodation they need and are commenting on photographs the agent is showing them. Encourage students to use the new housing vocabulary they have just learnt.

Tasks

Before listening

Arouse students' interest in the problems of finding somewhere to live by asking them where they would find advertisements, how difficult it is to find accommodation, if they would let a room in their home, etc. Then tell them it is difficult in England and set the scene for the tape by presenting the characters (Rod and Helen), telling them how difficult it is for Rod to find a flat, and presenting the relationship between the speakers (Helen is a friend of Rod's but not his girlfriend; Rod is married to Liz). Ask students to open their books at page 38 and to read the advertisements silently, but asking you any questions they may have.

Listening task

Tell students to listen first for the advantages and the disadvantages of each house or flat and to list them under the correct heading beside each advertisement. When they have done this they should listen again for the accommodation chosen and put a tick beside it. They should then try to answer the questions at the bottom. Let them check their answers together and with you. Round off the lesson by asking the students which house or flat they would like to rent and why.

Reading task

Present the fact that the British sell and buy things by putting postcards in shop windows. Present any new vocabulary or encourage students either to guess from the context or use a good dictionary to find what a word means. Check their comprehension by asking which number you should ring if, for example, you want to buy a boat. Then ask them what they notice about the language of this type of advertisement if they are advanced enough to profit from this kind of discussion. Point out the lack of verbs, subjects and prepositions.

Writing task

Tell students to copy items from the four cards printed to help them complete the blank cards. Before they start writing, encourage them to ask you for any words they need and are not sure of. They can write the cards either in class or for homework. Ideally, write one card with them in class and let them do the other one for homework. If they are not interested in the topics suggested for the blank cards, encourage them to think up topics of their own, but do not let them try anything too difficult in terms of vocabulary or too different from the cards printed.

Listening

List the advantages and disadvantages of the houses, flats etc. advertised. Tick the one chosen.

Answer the questions.

Advantages	**FLAT & HOUSE RENTALS**	*Disadvantages*
central	**ABINGDON** Road, single attic bedsitter and separate small kitchen £38 and £40 deposit, references. Tel. Oxford 774159	single
	ACCOMMODATION Kennington, suit non-smoking person. Tel. Oxford 739676 preferably 6.30 – 7.30 p.m.	for non-smoker, not very central
available immediately	**AVAILABLE** immediately. – Exceptionally attractive well appointed Cotswold House in isolated position 11 miles Oxford, 2 double bedrooms with bathrooms and dressing rooms ensuite, single bedroom, study, drawing room with dining area, large kitchen with laundry off, garden, car-port, stabling etc., long let preferred, £150 pcm. Tel. Witney 2554	11 miles from Oxford
available soon, suit young couple	**AVAILABLE SOON**, Furnished Flat, suitable young couple. – Tel. Oxford 40414	furnished
	BEDSITTING Room available now for lady, Summertown, limited use of kitchen, central heating, h and c water, prefer someone away on Sunday. –Tel. Oxford 55898	for lady
reasonable price	**BEDSIT** £14; Flat £28. ✓ Cottage £35.– Tel. Oxford 63785.	
central	**ROOM IN** shared House, £25 pw, central.– Tel. Oxford 724261	just one room

What kind of accommodation do these people really want?

For how many people? **2**

Number of bedrooms? **more than 1**

Maximum rent? **£30 per week**

How far from city centre? **not more than 2 or 3 miles**

Anything else? **must be allowed to smoke**

Reading and writing

You want to rent a holiday flat in Scotland for one week in August and to sell your electric cooker. Write the two postcards to put in your local shop window.

FREE TO A GOOD HOME !

Long-haired black kittens.
Very friendly, house-trained,
6 weeks old.
Tel: 395 6594

FOR SALE
LADIES' BICYCLE

Good condition, new
tyres, blue & white
£20
Mrs Davies 3 Southgate Rd

TO LET
Cottage in Cornwall. Sleeps 6,
in beautiful village, garden,
sea 2 miles

£50 per week

Ring 395 4028 after 6pm.

WANTED

Boat with motor for
family of 4.
No holes please !
Tel 395 3004 at weekends

WANTED
Holiday flat in Scotland.
1 Week in August (any other details)
(name and address/telephone number)

FOR SALE
ELECTRIC COOKER

Good condition, very
clean, white.
£20
(name and address/telephone number)

Objectives

1 To give students practice in determining a sequence of programmes from a discussion of one night's television.
2 To give students practice in reading and filling in a questionnaire.

Tape

Tapescript

Stuart: What did you do last night then? Did you work all night?
Judy: Yes, I did some work (Yes) but erm...I watched a bit of TV... (Uh-huh) got to relax, you know.
Stuart: Did you watch the football?
Judy: No, no I didn't. I can't bear football.
Stuart: Really?
Judy: Yes. (Coo) I really hate it. (Yes) Well, actually, just before the football came on, I switched over (Yes) just to...just to protest.
Stuart: What did you see then?
Judy: Well, I saw the programme before...just the end of a film (Uh-huh) that was on before the football. It looked quite good actually. It's a shame I didn't erm...switch on earlier. It was some kind of love story... with Dustin Hoffman, you know, the erm...
Stuart: *The Graduate*?
Judy: That's it, *The Graduate*.
Stuart: Yes. I know. I've seen that. (Yes) Yes, good...good film.
Judy: Yes, and nice music. (Mm-mm) And then, when the football came on I turned over.
Stuart: Terrible, terrible!
Judy: I hate it! I really can't stand it.
Stuart: It was a great game!
Judy: Yes? (What did) Who was playing?
Stuart: England, of course. (Oh) What did you see then, that was more important than football?
Judy: Foxes. Yes, a good programme on foxes. (Uh-huh) Yes, they spent ages watching these foxes in a house. (Yes) They were watching them all night and these little baby foxes...it was tremendous.
Stuart: Yes, sounds all right.
Judy: Yes, it was good; better than football...and then, then I turned over, back to the other channel (Mm-mm) to see who won the football, but I

missed it and I just saw the beginning of the News and packed up and went to bed.

Stuart: Well, I'm sorry you missed it. It was a good game.
Judy: Who did win?
Stuart: England, of course. Who do you think? (Ah) Six nil. (Yes) Yes.
Judy: Must have been quite good then!
Stuart: Yes, it was good, actually. It was very good. (Mm)

Length: 1 min. 34 sec.
Number of speakers: 2.
Setting: Two friends talking at work one morning.

Key language

Function: Expressing likes and dislikes in relation to one night's television programmes.

Lexis:
TV	turn over
football	fox
switch over	baby
end (noun)	channel
love story	news
graduate	

Structures: I can't bear...
I really hate...
it looked quite good
it's a shame I didn't...
I really can't stand...
more...than
it was...
(it) sounds...
better than...
I'm sorry you missed...
(it) must have been...

TEACHING HINTS

Teach any new structures of liking, disliking and preferring in the context of television programmes in general and the students' own preferences. Then teach any new lexis in the context of a real or imaginary evening's viewing. Make sure that you introduce the idea of having more than one channel to choose from.

Tasks

Before listening

Tell your students that there are three channels in England: BBC1, BBC2 and ITV. Explain that the first two (British Broadcasting Corporation channels) are financed by the government and that ITV is independant, relying for a large part of its income on advertising. Then ask them to open their books at page 40 and look at the types of programme illustrated. Ask them to identify each one and say which ones they would have chosen to watch. Set the scene for the tape by introducing the characters Stuart and Judy who work together. Tell them that they are going to hear a conversation between these two just after they have arrived at work one morning.

Listening task

Tell students to listen and identify the programmes Judy watched. They then listen again and write down the programmes in the blank TV screens in the order in which they appeared. Let them check their answers with each other and then with you. Ask them if they would have watched the football or the programme on foxes.

Reading task

Encourage students to talk about specific programmes they like or dislike. Then ask them to find out about the preferences, likes and dislikes of the person sitting next to them. Give them a few minutes to do this and then ask some students to tell you about their colleagues. Ask the students to open their books and read the questionnaire, checking what the types of programme mean by looking at the examples printed down the sides of the page. Answer any queries.

Writing task

Give students as long as necessary to complete the questionnaire about themselves. Talk about their answers briefly and then ask them to find out the opinions of three other people in the room. When they have done this, talk about their findings and ask them to begin to generalise about the class's opinions of various programmes. At this point they can either collate all their findings to draw up a class survey of the popularity of television programmes (you can help them collate their information on the blackboard) or for homework they can write a simple report of their own findings.

Listening

In the three blank TVs show which programmes the girl watched. In TV number 1 write the first programme, in 2 the second and in 3 the third.
Which programmes were on the same channel?

Reading and writing

TV Questionnaire

1. Do you like these types of programmes or not? (Tick or cross)

	You	Student 1	Student 2	Student 3	Total ✓	Total ✗
Films	✓	✓	✓	✓	4	0
News & current affairs	✓	✗	✓	✗	2	2
Discussion						
Sport						
Music						
Comedy						
Serials						
Crime						
Plays						
Documentary						
Other:						

2. What is your favourite programme?
   You: e.g. Starsky and Hutch
   Student 1:
   Student 2:
   Student 3:

3. What programme do you like least?
   You: e.g. The News
   Student 1:
   Student 2:
   Student 3:

4. What would you like more of?
   You: e.g. Music
   Student 1:
   Student 2:
   Student 3:

5. What would you like less of?
   You: e.g. Sport
   Student 1:
   Student 2:
   Student 3:

Crime:
Starsky and Hutch

Music:
**Mozart's
'The Marriage of Figaro**

Comedy:
Laugh with Larry

Play:
Hamlet

Sport:
World Cup Football

Film:
High Noon

Discussion:
**Expert Ideas on the
Oil Crisis**

Documentary:
The Sahara Desert

News and current affairs
Tonight

Discussion:
**For and Against
Nuclear Power**

Music:
Top of the Pops

Documentary:
Life on Earth

Serial:
**Dickens's
'David Copperfield'**

Play:
Macbeth

Comedy:
Laurel and Hardy

Crime:
Kojak

Film:
Star Wars

Objectives

1 To help students understand and follow a conversation between three people who are deciding what film to see.
2 To give students practice in reading a brochure about the Royal Shakespeare Company's forthcoming programme and in booking seats by post.

Tape

Tapescript

Diana: Well, are we going to go out tonight, then?

Mary: Yes. Good idea! (Mm) What shall we do?

Dick: Let's go to the pictures.

Diana: Yes, that would be quite nice.

Mary: Oh, is Ray coming?

Diana: Well, he said if we went to see a film, he'd definitely be coming, yes.

Mary: OK, so what's on?

Dick: Mm...I've been to the one at Walton Street. I went last week and I think they've got *Annie Hall* and *Star Wars*, I think. (Mm) I think *Annie Hall's* on at 8 o'clock (Yes) and *Star Wars* is on at quarter to 8, I think it is.

Mary: Quarter to 8.

Dick: Yes, I think it's £1.

Mary: Ah. Uh-huh. £1 to get in?

Diana: Well, I've seen *Annie Hall* twice, you see, already (Mm) so I'd rather see something else. D'you know the Odeon?

Dick: In the Cowley Road?

Diana: Yes, that's right.

Mary: Oh, I know, yes, and it's really cheap to get in, isn't it?

Diana: Yes, it's only 50p.

Mary: Uh-huh.

Diana: Well, they're showing *Yellow Submarine*.

Mary: W...What time?

Dick: Oh, I've seen it.

Diana: Oh, what a pity.

Diana: Well, we would have had a choice of performances, either 7 o'clock (No) or 9 o'clock.

Dick: I really don't want to go and see that again. I've seen it on the television as well.

Diana: Don't you like the Beatles, Dick?

Dick: Well yes, but it's sort of ten years ago, isn't it?

Mary: Oh.

Diana: Oh. OK.

Mary: So, well what about the Palace. D'you know it? It's in...er...George Street – (Mm) because they've got *The Deer Hunter* on there.

Diana: *The Deer Hunter*? What's that?

Mary: Well, it's about American soldiers coming back from Vietnam. S'posed to be really good, and it starts at 8.30, but the only problem is, it may be a little bit expensive – ... £1.30.

Dick: It's violent though, isn't it?

Mary: Well, I mean...not too violent. What d'you think? And we could meet, you see, we could meet Ray in the pub. There's a pub opposite – more or less opposite.

Diana: Shall we meet earlier (Yes) at the pub?

Dick: Then we can have a drink.

Mary: Yes, OK. What does it...? So it starts at 8.30. (Mm)

Dick: Half past 7. Meet at half past 7.

Mary: All right. Meet in the pub half past 7.

Diana: OK, yes. Well, what shall I tell Ray? What if he can't make the pub at half past 7?

Mary: Well, if he can't make the pub, then he could meet us outside, half past 8.

Diana: OK, right. I'll let him know.

Length: 2 min. 5 sec.
Number of speakers: 3.
Setting: Three friends at home deciding what film to see that evening.

Key language

Function: Asking for and making suggestions, and giving information about cinema programmes.

Lexis:
the Odeon	really cheap
the Palace	expensive
to get in	That's a good idea
to meet	That'd be quite nice
pub	

Structures:
What shall we do...?	They're showing...
What about...?	They've got ... on.
Let's ...?	It's on at...
We could ...	It starts at...
I'd rather ...	opposite...
I don't want to ...	outside...
What's on?	

TEACHING HINTS

First check that students are familiar with alternative ways of expressing the time, e.g. 7.45 = a quarter to 8. Cut out entertainment advertisements from your local paper, make up your own or ask students to make them up. The advertisement should include the name of a film or play, times of performances and seat prices. Use these advertisements to introduce some of the responses to the question

'What shall we do...?' Then introduce the phrases of agreement and disagreement. Finally introduce the question 'What's on?' and practise the ways of giving information about the film, times of performances and cost.

Tasks

Before listening

Ask students to open their books at page 42 and look at the names of the four films. Ask if anyone has seen any of the films or knows what they are about. Encourage them to talk about these films, e.g. who the actors are, whether it is fact or fiction. If nobody has seen these particular films they are almost certain to have seen one which aroused their interest and which they could talk about. Tell students they are going to listen to three friends talking about films.

Listening task

Ask students to look at the four advertisements and work out which information they have to listen for and fill in. Note that the name of the cinema has been filled in for *Annie Hall* and *Star Wars*. (It is quite common in England for one building to house a number of 'screens' showing different programmes.)

When students have filled in the information on the advertisements ask them to complete the message for Ray. Make sure they read the message right through before beginning to fill it in. Let them check their answers with each other then with you.

Reading task

Some students who have visited England will probably have visited Stratford and the Royal Shakespeare Theatre. If so, ask them to tell the others about the place and the theatre. Ask students to read the instructions carefully: 'You want to book ... ... would also be all right.' Then tell them to look at the booking form to see what information they have to find. Firstly, they have to find the date which suits them best and an alternative date. Direct them to the 'Performance schedule' and tell them to ring the appropriate dates. Next direct them towards 'Please note' to find out which performances are matinée and which evening. In order to fill in the 'Price' ask students to look at the plan of the layout of the theatre. If they understand 'Stage' they can probably deduce the meaning of 'stall', 'circle', 'balcony' and 'box'. Finally they have to decide which seats they can afford.

Writing task

Ask students to read carefully 'How to use this form' and then to try to fill it in. Before starting check that they know what block letters are, what 'For office use only' means and how to deal with questions they cannot answer, e.g. Membership No.

When students have finished go round and check their answers making sure they have booked seats for the right performance and as far as possible at the right price.

Listening

Fill in the missing information on the advertisements. Then complete the message for Ray.

CINEMA: **THE CONTINENTAL SCREEN 1**
Annie Hall
TIME: 8.00
PRICE: £1.00

CINEMA: **The Odeon**
Yellow Submarine
TIME: 7.00 9.00
PRICE: 50p

CINEMA: **THE CONTINENTAL SCREEN 2**
STAR WARS
TIME: 7.45
PRICE: £1.00

CINEMA: **The Palace**
The Deer Hunter
TIME: 8.30
PRICE: £1.30

Ray
We're going to see 'The Deer Hunter'
at _8.30_ . See you outside
the _Palace_ cinema or in
the pub opposite.
Love from Dick, Diana, Mary

Reading and writing

You want to book two tickets for *Julius Caesar* for a Friday evening in October, but any Saturday in October would also be all right. Fill in the booking form below.

Royal Shakespeare Company
Stratford-upon-Avon
Performance Schedule

Sat 29 Sep 7.30	J CAESAR	
Mon 1 Oct 7.30	J CAESAR	
Tue 2 Oct 6.30*pn*	J CAESAR	
Wed 3 Oct 7.30	J CAESAR	
Thu 4 Oct 7.30	MERRY WIVES	
Fri 5 Oct 7.30	OTHELLO	
Sat 6 Oct 2.00*m*	TWELFTH NGT	
Sat 6 Oct 7.30	CYMBELINE	
Mon 8 Oct 7.30	CYMBELINE	
Tue 9 Oct 7.30	J CAESAR	
Wed 10 Oct 7.30	J CAESAR	
Thu 11 Oct 2.00*m*	TWELFTH NGT	
Thu 11 Oct 7.30	MERRY WIVES	
Fri 12 Oct 7.30	J CAESAR	
Sat 13 Oct 1.30*m*	OTHELLO	
Sat 13 Oct 7.30	TWELFTH NGT	
Mon 15 Oct 7.30	J CAESAR	
Tue 16 Oct 7.30	TWELFTH NGT	
Wed 17 Oct 7.30	OTHELLO	
Thu 18 Oct 2.00*m*	J CAESAR	
Thu 18 Oct 7.30	J CAESAR	
Fri 19 Oct 7.30	CYMBELINE	
Sat 20 Oct 2.00*m*	MERRY WIVES	
Sat 20 Oct 7.30	OTHELLO	
Mon 22 Oct 7.30	MERRY WIVES	
Tue 23 Oct 7.30	J CAESAR	
Wed 24 Oct 7.30	TWELFTH NGT	
Thu 25 Oct 2.00*m*	TWELFTH NGT	
Thu 25 Oct 7.30	CYMBELINE	
Fri 26 Oct 7.30	OTHELLO	
Sat 27 Oct 2.00*m*	MERRY WIVES	
Sat 27 Oct 7.30	J CAESAR	
Mon 29 Oct 7.30	TWELFTH NGT	
Tue 30 Oct 7.30	MERRY WIVES	
Wed 31 Oct 7.30	J CAESAR	
Thu 1 Nov 2.00*m*	J CAESAR	
Thu 1 Nov 7.30	TWELFTH NGT	
Fri 2 Nov 7.30	OTHELLO	
Sat 3 Nov 2.00*m*	MERRY WIVES	
Sat 3 Nov 7.30	CYMBELINE	

Please note: the performances on 7 August and 2 October start at 6.30 pm, and the matinee performances on 8, 13, 15, 20 September and 13 October start at 1.30 pm. Performance details are published in good faith but changes may occasionally be necessary.
pn = press night
m = matinee
p = preview*
c = concert
*Revisions may be made to a production following its first performance. For this reason this performance is designated a preview.

Julius Caesar

New Production
Cast includes:
Peter Clough — *Octavius*
Ben Kingsley — *Brutus*
James Laurenson — *Cassius*
Nigel Terry — *Casca*
David Threlfall — *Mark Antony*
John Woodvine — *Julius Caesar*
Director — Barry Kyle
Designer — Christopher Morley

Music — James Walker
Lighting — Brian Harris

Shakespeare wrote *Julius Caesar* in 1599 and it was one of the first plays that his company, The Lord Chamberlain's Men, presented at their new Globe Theatre in the same year. It was a favourite until the closing of the theatres in 1642 and was acted several times at Court.

Press reviews will first appear on 3 October.

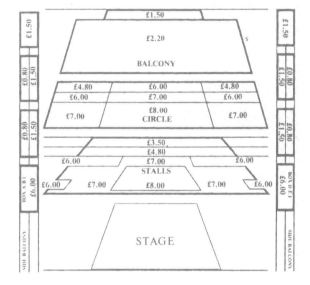

How to use this form: Complete the form in block letters giving alternative dates and prices where possible. If you are paying by cheque please make it payable to the Royal Shakespeare Theatre, *but leave the actual amount open, stating only an upper limit.* Please send completed form (having checked that dates correspond to performances of play you require) with remittance to the Box Office, Royal Shakespeare Theatre, Stratford-upon-Avon, Warwickshire CV37 6BB. *Remember to enclose stamped addressed envelope.*

I apply for the tickets entered below and have given alternative dates and prices.

I enclose s.a.e. and an open cheque limited to the value of £ 14.00

Please note discount for members of the RSC Mailing List has now been discontinued.

Full/Associate Membership No.	NONE
Name	JEREMY WILDE
Address	115 OFFMORE ROAD
	WORCESTER

Tel. Home 773061	Tel. Business —
Date 1 AUG 1981	

Date 1st choice	Matinee or Evening	Alternative Dates	Matinee or Evening	Number of Tickets	Price	Alternative Prices	OFFICE USE ONLY
Fri 12 Oct.	Evening	Sat 27 Oct.	Evening	2	£6	£7	

107

22 Guessing what people are talking about

Objectives

1 To help students to infer the topic of conversation by listening to a short extract of it.
2 To help students infer the source of a number of written extracts and to fill in a form asking for specific information.

Tape

Note: There are four extracts recorded for this unit. They are numbered 1,2,3,4, and are self-sufficient. You can, therefore, choose whether to do all four or any one, two or three of them.

Tapescript 1

Fiona: OK Deek, I'm off now. (OK) Everything's OK, is it?
Deek: Yes, I think so, erm...the only thing is... is she likely to wake up?
Fiona: No, I don't think so. She doesn't usually, but...
Deek: What if she does?
Fiona: Well, yes. Don't worry about it. Her dummy's by the bed, so if you just pick her up (Yes) give her the dummy, give her a little bit of a cuddle, (Yes) sing to her if you like.
Deek: Shall I read her a story or something?
Fiona: Yes, anything like that. (Yes) Erm... then she should just go back to sleep again quite happily.
Deek: OK.
Fiona: Oh! And I've left stuff for you in the fridge. There's some salad and cold chicken and some beer as well. OK then?
Deek: Right-ho then. Bye.
Fiona: Bye.

Length: 30 sec.
Number of speakers: 2.
Setting: A young mother is leaving instructions with her babysitter before going out for the evening.

Key language

Function: Telling someone how to look after a baby.

Lexis: go back to sleep   sing
      wake up   story
      cuddle

Structures: give her ...

             sing to her

Tapescript 2

Lesley:	Ah...it's such a lovely day. It reminds me of last week, doesn't it you?
Fiona:	Oh don't! I mean that was just so fantastic, that holiday!
Lesley:	I love that city, you know.
Fiona:	I do too. Really, it's got something about it, a certain sort of charm...
Lesley:	Mm, and all that wine and good food...
Fiona:	And so cheap. Right, I mean, compared to here...
Lesley:	Yes, although the shops are expensive.
Fiona:	Mm, yes.
Lesley:	I mean, really I bought nothing at all. I just ate and ate and drank and drank.
Fiona:	I know. Wasn't that lovely?
Lesley:	Yes. And, I don't know, I like listening to the people talking and sitting outside drinking wine and...
Fiona:	Yes. Could you understand what they were saying? When they were speaking quickly, I mean.
Lesley:	Well, it is difficult, of course. And then I liked that tower, too.
Fiona:	You liked that tower? I'm not sure about it, really. (No) It's very unusual, right in the centre of the city.
Lesley:	True, but there's a lovely view from the top.
Fiona:	Oh, you went right up, didn't you? (Mm, yes) Oh no, I didn't.
Lesley:	Of course you didn't.
Fiona:	I remember that day. We weren't together.
Lesley:	No, that's right. (Mm) You went down by the river, didn't you?
Fiona:	That's it. Oh, walking along the river and all the couples (Yes) and it's so romantic... (Is it true) and the paintings too...
Lesley:	They do have artists down by the river, do they? (Yes) Oh, how lovely!
Fiona:	Oh, it really is super.
Lesley:	Yes. Oh, I think we ought to go back there again next year, don't you?
Fiona:	I do, yes. (Mm) If only just to sample some more of the wine.
Lesley:	It'd be lovely, wouldn't it?
Fiona:	Yes.

Length: 1 min. 5 sec.

Number of speakers: 2.

Setting: Two friends are sitting outside a pub talking about their holiday together in Paris.

Key language

Function: Talking about past events.

Lexis:	holiday	expensive
	city	tower
	wine	view
	good food	paintings
	cheap	

Structures: I love ...
I like ...
I remember...
It reminds...of...

Tapescript 3

Mrs Hunt: I thought I could hear this noise so eventually I managed to wake up
and... you wouldn't believe (What?) well...erm... he hadn't pu...fixed
the clip tight enough (Oh) and the tap was under pressure. (Dear)
Three ceilings down!
Mrs Jacks: Oh how awful.
Mrs Hunt: And it was all pouring away, absolutely dreadful you wouldn't
believe. I couldn't even find out where to turn it off at the beginning
because you know new houses and all that (Yes) so in the end I
managed to turn it off and then the mopping up. It took me half the
night. Three ceilings down. Got to have it all redecorated.
Mrs Jacks: Well you must make him do something about it. (Yes, well...) my
goodness, get on to him straightaway.
Mrs Hunt: OK. Well yes I'm going to.
Mrs Jacks: Good.

Length: 27 sec.
Number of speakers: 2.
Setting: Two friends chatting together. One is telling how the plumber had
caused her washing machine to flood and damage three ceilings.

Key language

Function: Telling a story about a terrible event.

Lexis:
noise	pouring
wake up	mopping up
tap	redecorate
ceilings	turn off

Tapescript 4

Mrs Hunt: Anyway I...I'm so pleased. What about you then?
Mrs Jacks: Well, he said he wanted to have another look at it.
Mrs Hunt: Yes. What are they doing about it?
Mrs Jacks: Well, I don't think they're going to do anything really. It just
sometimes goes away (Well can't...) something like that.
Mrs Hunt: Well, can't they give you anything for it?
Mrs Jacks: Well no, they didn't say they could. (Really?) No, just got to be
patient and wait for it to go away.
Mrs Hunt: Well, that seems a bit stupid, doesn't it?
Mrs Jacks: Yes it does.
Mrs Hunt: You'd have thought... You'd have thought they'd have thought of
something.
Mrs Jacks: Yes. Ooh it's your turn.

110

Mrs Hunt: Oh yes, so it is. Well, Cheerio...
Mrs Jacks: Good luck.
Mrs Hunt: Thank you...

Length: 45 sec.
Number of speakers: 2.
Setting: Two friends meeting at the doctor's surgery.

Key language

Function: Talking about what is wrong with you.

Lexis: patient   it's your turn
       wait for   go away

Structures: do something about ...
           give ... for...

TEACHING HINTS

Since the objective of this unit is to give students help and practice in inferring what people are talking about from extracts of their conversations it would 'give the game away' to teach the above key language since this would enable the student to do the task without even hearing the tape.

Tasks

Before listening

Ask students to open their books at page 44 and to look at the six cartoons there. Ask them to say what is happening in each of them. Feed in as much of the key language as appropriate and other items for those cartoons not on the tape.

Listening task

Tell students they are going to hear an extract of a conversation which is depicted in one of the six cartoons. Play the first extract and ask students to write 1 beside the picture depicting the topic of the conversation. Play the tape again and ask them to write down the words they heard which brought them to that conclusion.

This procedure may be repeated for all four extracts if you choose to do so. The four are graded in degree of difficulty. Number 4 being the most difficult since there are few key words to latch on to.

Reading task

Just as students inferred the topic of a conversation by listening to a short extract and latching onto the key words so in the reading task students infer where the written extracts come from. Therefore, at the beginning discourage explanations of unknown vocabulary and the use of dictionaries and encourage students to read the extracts and fill in the boxes underneath with the place they came from. Then ask them to ring the key words which brought them to these conclusions. If students find this very difficult write up a list of places where the extracts might come from.

Writing task

The student identity card is an example of the kind of form students may have to fill out in English. Check that students know the difference between 'name' and 'forename' and 'signature'. The 'Educational Establishment' is the one they are studying at. 'Valid until' could be one year from now or the date when their studies finish.

It is worth pointing out that information of this sort is usually written in block capitals (except the signature, of course.)

Completed listening task

Listening

Put number 1 in the box beside the cartoon which illustrates the first conversation.
Make a list of the important words which helped you reach this conclusion.
Do the same for conversations 2, 3 and 4.

have another look

wait for it to go away

give you something for it

your turn

city
wine
good food
tower
river
paintings

wake up

cuddle

story

go back to sleep

noise

tap

pouring

mopping up

three ceilings down

redecorate

Reading and writing

Write down where you would expect to see these.

Directions. Empty contents of a packet of Sainsbury's Blancmange Powder into a 1½ pint basin. From a pint of milk take enough to mix the powder to a smooth paste. Boil the remainder of the milk with 2 tablespoonfuls of sugar. Pour onto the mixture stirring well. Return to saucepan and boil for two minutes stirring all the time. Pour into wetted mould and leave to set.

food packet

I E GULLIKSON and I R GUL-
LIKSON (US) beat O Bengston
(Sweden) and R Fisher (US) 7—5, 7—5,
6—2; R J Carmichael (Australia) and
Teacher (US) beat V L Eke (Australia)
and W J Farrel (GB) 6—3, 7—6, 6—4,
C S Dibley and B D Drewett
(Australia) beat B Manson and A I
Pattison (US) 6—7, 6—3, 6—2, 3—6,
10—8.

Sports section of newspaper

Completed writing

newspaper

2   DESCRIPTION *SIGNALEMENT*

	Bearer Titulaire	Spouse Epouse
Occupation Profession		
Place of birth Lieu de naissance		
Date of birth Date de naissance		
Residence Résidence		
Height Taille	m	m
Distinguishing marks Signes particuliers		

CHILDREN *ENFANTS*

Name Nom	Date of birth Date de naissance	Sex Sexe

Usual signature of bearer
Signature du titulaire

Usual signature of spouse
Signature de son epouse

passport

English Beef

Mince per lb ———————— **56p**

Boneless Roasting (back rib) per lb **£1.02**

English Pork

Boneless Roasting (shoulder) per lb ———— **79p**

Provisions Counter

Freshly Sliced Danish Prime Unsmoked Middle Cut Rashers per lb **78p**

Freshly Cut Imported Cheddar Cheese per lb ———— **69p**

Freshly Cut Dutch Edam Cheese per lb ———— **59p**

supermarket window/newspaper advert.

Fill in this identity card for yourself in block letters.

STUDENT IDENTITY CARD

ATTACH PHOTO. HERE	DATE OF BIRTH **14.2.60**	
	NAME **WILLIAMS**	N° A 489491
	FORENAME **STEPHEN**	
	NATIONALITY **BRITISH**	
	S. Williams SIGNATURE	

EDUCATIONAL ESTABLISHMENT **WATFORD COLLEGE OF EDUCATION**

VALID UNTIL **JULY 1982**

PLACE AND DATE **WATFORD SEPT. '80**

Add the chicken meat and still stirring cook for four minutes more. Stir in the ginger, soy sauce, sherry, pepper, salt and 12 fluid ounces (1½ cups) of the chicken stock. Reduce the heat to low and simmer for forty minutes. Stir in the cornflour paste and simmer for two minutes. Add the cream, stir well and cook for one minute more.

recipe book

Objectives

1 To give students practice in following instructions given to someone learning a sport and then in inferring what that sport is.
2 To give students practice in following basic written instructions and in writing similar instructions of their own.

Tape

Note: There are three extracts recorded for this unit. They are numbered 1,2,3, and are self-sufficient. You can, therefore, choose whether to do all three or any one or two of them.

Tapescript 1

Steve: Good. Now then ...er... lift the club backwards away from the ball. (Mm) That's it. Keeping that left arm straight...
Fern: Mm. It's not easy.
Steve: ... till you get to the top of the swing. (Yes) Good. Now the very important thing – you must keep your head down all the time.
Fern: Down?
Steve: Yes, keep looking at the ball.
Fern: Oh but I'm looking at the club.
Steve: No. You must look at the ball. That's it. Right, now...
Fern: It's not a very natural position, is it?
Steve: Well, now swing down. (Yes) That's it... swing down and through (Mm) keeping that left arm straight (Yes) and even when you... even after you've hit the ball you must keep that head looking at where the ball was. Yes.
Fern: It doesn't seem right to me!
Steve: No. No. You're doing really well. That's OK.
Fern: It's not easy, is it?
Steve: And after you've hit the ball keep looking at where the ball was (Mm) but make sure you throw that club towards the hole.
Fern: That's not going to be difficult at all. I've almost let go several times.
Steve: You mustn't let go. I mean you must just point the club towards the hole.
Fern: Yes, that's why I'm looking in that direction so I can check where it's gone... hasn't gone very far actually.
Steve: Good. You'll be really good.

Length: 50 sec.
Number of speakers: 2.
Setting: A golf course.

Key language

Function: Giving instructions.

Lexis: lift   straight
       backwards   swing
       arm

Structures: lift ...
            keeping ... straight
            you must/mustn't...
            keep ...ing

Tapescript 2

Tom: Am I standing in the right position?
Ruth: Well, you've got to bend your knees a bit more... and thrust your hands back, so when you go into the water, you make your head follow, er... go straight in and your legs follow.
Tom: Is this OK?
Ruth: Yes, that's just...yes, that's just about right and bend your knees a little bit more.
Tom: Does...? This all right now?
Ruth: Yes, that's fine. Now, put your hands back, behind your back. OK? Nice and straight...yes, that's it, and then, make it...now, go on, go! Make your head go straight in and your, erm...legs follow.

Length: 30 sec.
Number of speakers: 2.
Setting: The edge of a swimming pool.

Key language

Function: Giving instructions.

Lexis: bend   legs
       knees   follow
       thrust back   straight
       head

Structures: you've got to...
            thrust...
            bend... a little bit more
            make your ... go...

Tapescript 3

Jackie: Lesley, I don't think it likes me!
Lesley: Oh, never mind Jackie, now relax. Now take a deep breath (Uh) all right, because it can sense if you're nervous. (OK) All right? (Mm) Now, you feeling OK? (Yes) Jolly good. Now, take your left hand, (Mm-mm) and get some hair on its neck...(Mm) get a good firm hold. (OK) Now, can you lift your left leg and put it in the stirrup...you put your foot in

the stirrup. (My left leg) OK? Yes. Hang on tight with your left hand on...(Uh-huh) onto the hair. OK? (Right) And put your left foot in the stirrup.

Jackie: Fine. So my toes are pointing forwards?

Lesley: No, your toes are facing towards its back...end. (Ah) All right? (OK.Mm) OK? Right, now, can you hop round (Mm-mm) so that you're facing its middle (Mm-mm) Alright? And put your other hand on the back of the saddle. (Fine) OK? Feeling comfortable? (Yes) OK. Now, you've got to take a big jump, and you've got to swing your leg over the back, but don't kick it, because it'll be frightened. (Uh-huh-huh-huh) OK?

Jackie: *It*'ll be frightened? OK, here we go.

Length: 40 sec.
Number of speakers: 2.
Setting: An open field.

Key language

Function: Giving instructions.

Lexis:

left hand	back
hair	hop
neck	middle
lift	jump
leg	swing over
toes	kick
forwards	

Structures: relax
take...
can you lift...
hop...so that you're...
don't kick...

TEACHING HINTS

Teach lexis and structures in the context of a keep fit class. Devise simple exercises that you can demonstrate while presenting the key language and that your students can then act out and practise. For example, 'Lift your arms in the air... straight in the air. Now swing them forwards and backwards' etc. Note that you need only prepare for one sport at a time. Then ask students to make up their own exercises and give a partner or the class instructions to make them do them. Do not present such items as 'ball', 'club' and 'hole' as they should be deduced from the context and to teach them would make the listening task too easy.

Tasks

Before listening

Ask students what sports they like or can do and what sports they would like to learn. Supply vocabulary where necessary. Then ask them to think of their first lesson in a sport they know and try to remember what it was like. Ask specific questions, e.g. 'Was it difficult?', 'Was it boring?' etc. Then ask them to imagine a first lesson in a sport they can't do and which would be difficult, e.g. ski-ing, water ski-ing, or karate. Elicit from them what they think it would be like. Then tell them that they are going to listen to a first lesson and ask them to open their books at page 46.

Listening task

Play the first extract and ask students to write 1 beside the picture depicting the sport being taught. Play the tape again and ask students to write down the words which brought them to that conclusion.

This procedure may be repeated for all three extracts if you choose to do so.

Once students have identified the sport, help them to deduce from the context the meaning of such words as 'saddle', 'hole' and 'club'.

If it helps and the classroom layout allows, students can get up and act out the instructions to help them follow them. To round the lesson off, students can give each other instructions for sports they know and guess the sports concerned.

Reading task

Ask students to look at the pictures on page 47 and guess what they are illustrating (yoga). Then find out if anyone practises or has practised yoga and what the class think of it. Ask them, without looking at the text, to devise instructions to accompany picture 4. Help them as much as necessary and then tell them to read instructions A silently. When they have read them, answer any queries and ask whether they go with picture 4 (no). Then ask which picture they go with (3). Then ask students to read instructions B and C and decide which pictures they accompany.

Writing task

Ask students orally to make up instructions for picture 2. Practise these thoroughly and then ask students to write them in the space provided either in class or for homework.

23 Following instructions

Listening

Which sport is being taught in the first conversation? Put number 1 in the box beside the photo. Make a list of the important words which helped you reach this conclusion. Do the same for conversations 2 and 3.

Skate-boarding ☐

Squash ☐

Riding 3

Diving 2

bend .... knees
water
hands back
behind ... back
head
legs follow

Golf 1

Surfing ☐

1

2

3

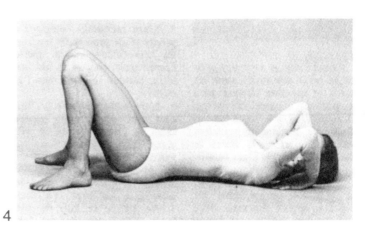

4

Match three of the above pictures (1, 2, 3 or 4) with the instructions below
(A, B, or C). Write the correct numbers in the boxes below and then write
instructions to go with the other picture.

| 3 | A Kneel on the floor. Lean back and hold your legs just above the ankles with each hand. Keep your arms straight. Look up. |

| 4 | B Lie with your knees bent and your feet flat on the floor. Put your hands flat on the floor on either side of your head. Keep your head on the floor and look up. |

| 1 | C Put your hands and feet flat on the floor. Raise your body as high in the air as possible, with your knees bent a little but your arms straight. Look down at the floor. |

| 2 | D Stand with your feet apart. Lean back and hold the back of your ankles with each hand, with your knees bent a little. Look up. |

Objectives

1 To give students practice in following narrative and in appreciating the point of a funny story.
2 To give students the chance to write a caption for a cartoon and so create a written joke in English.

Tape

Tapescript

Lesley: Oh Jackie, I've had such a terrible day.

Jackie: You look exhausted. What on earth have you been doing?

Lesley: Oh, I've been such a fool! (Oh) You just wouldn't believe what I've done.

Jackie: I would, I would. Come on... (You won't) Where've you been?

Lesley: I'm dying to tell someone. I've been down to London (Uh-huh) you see. (Uh-huh) OK, I thought I'd be very sensible, so I'd drive down to the Underground on...on the outskirts of London, leave the car and go in by Tube. All right? (Er...what you) Very sensible. (Yes) Yes? (OK) OK. So I drove down to London (Uh-huh) and I parked my car by the Tube station and I got the Tube into London. (Uh-huh) Fine! All right? (Well, sounds like it) so far, so good. (Yes) Right. Came back out of London ... (Uh-huh...and you er...forgot the car?) Got out of the Tube. No, no, I didn't forget the car. (Oh) I couldn't find the car, Jackie. (You're joking) It'd gone. (You're kidding) No, no, really, it'd gone. I walked out... happily out of the Tube, you know, over to where it was (Mm) and I looked and it was a red Mini and mine's green, so (Oh no!) I thought 'Oh no'. So having panicked a bit, I rang the police, you see, and this lovely, new little policeman ... a young one (Yes, all shiny and bright) came out to help. That's it yes...buttons shining... (Yes) big smile...came down to help, so I said 'I've lost my car. It's been stolen' and I took him to see it and everything and...

Jackie: You mean where it wasn't.

Lesley: And sure enough, it wasn't...yes, well, right... and it wasn't there. And then he coughed a bit and he went very quiet... (Oh dear) and he took me back into the Tube station (Oh dear) and out the other side into the other car park...and there was my car, Jackie (Oh Lesley) parked in the other Tube station car park, the other side of the station, because there are two exits, you see, so I walked out of an exit (Yes) not knowing there were two and it was in the other one.

Jackie: Oh Lesley. And was he ever so cross?

Lesley: He was livid, Jackie. (Really) He really...he went on and on at me and I didn't know what to do. It was (Oh dear) just frightful. I just...I went red and just shut up and said 'Sorry' all the time.

Jackie: Jumped in your car and (Oh yes) and left.

Lesley: Oh, it was awful. I'm never doing that again ever.

Length: 2 min. 1 sec.

Number of speakers: 2.

Setting: Someone telling a friend about the very bad day she has just had.

Key language

Function: Narrating events.

Lexis: Underground   exit
leave   livid
Tube   go on and on at
cough (verb)   go red
quiet   shut up

Structures: I've been down to...
I thought I'd ...
I drove...
I didn't forget...
I couldn't find...
it'd gone.
I've lost ...
it's been stolen
he took me...
there was...
I'm never doing that again

TEACHING HINTS

Use this extract to revise past tenses. Practise them by telling the students a funny or exciting story of your own. Present the transport items in the context of travelling around London, e.g. 'You leave your car at the Tube station and go in by Tube.'

Tasks

Before listening

Tell students they are going to hear a conversation between two friends, Jackie and Lesley. Lesley has just arrived home from a terrible trip to London and tells Jackie about it. Tell students to open their books at page 48 and study the four cartoons, looking particularly for the differences between them.

Listening task

Tell students to keep looking at the cartoons while the tape is being played and to select the cartoon that illustrates Lesley's story most accurately and put a tick beside it. When they have identified the correct cartoon (3), ask them why it is the correct one and thus elicit the point of the story. Encourage students to tell funny stories of their own. Practise such utterances as 'I've been dying to tell someone', 'You're kidding' and 'I'm never doing that again' intensively so that students can use them in their own stories. Make sure the rest of the class commiserate with them as the friend did in the extract.

Writing task

Now ask students to look at the cartoons on page 49. Take the middle cartoon first and as a class think up a caption for the notice. Set the scene by asking whether they are good children, how the father is feeling and why they think the old man looks so worried. Then repeat the process with the other two cartoons, asking which birds are nice and which nasty, what the dove is carrying, if the man and the woman in the balloon are man and wife, how he/she feels etc. Do this as a class and do not set it as homework as it is much more fun when done by a group.

24   Parking in London

Listening

Tick the cartoon which illustrates the story most accurately.

Reading and writing

What do you think they are saying?
Complete the cartoons in your own words.

This is a highjack!

Take your hands off me, young man!

Note: These are only examples of possible answers.

25 Doing puzzles

Objectives

1 To give students practice in identifying people and locations.
2 To give students the chance to solve a written English puzzle.

Tape

Tapescript

Jackie: Hi Lesley! You look as if you're having fun. What are you doing?

Lesley: Well, yes, I'm trying to do these puzzles, Jackie (Ah) and I just can't do them.

Jackie: Exactly the kind of thing I like doing. Let's have a look.

Lesley: Erm...have a look at this face. Now, who d'you think that is? Look (Erm) he's not English, is he?

Jackie: No. He's definitely someone famous. Now let me think... er...is he an actor?

Lesley: Well, no. I don't think so. (Isn't he) I thought of Omar Sharif, but it's not Omar Sharif (Ah) is it? (Could be) But it's someone from that part of the world, I think.

Jackie: Oh, come on. Who is it?

Lesley: It's King Hussein of Jordan.

Jackie: Oh! Of course!

Lesley: Now, the one I really haven't looked at is...is the one at the bottom.

Jackie: Ah. Ah. Yes, find ten differences...have you found any?

Lesley: No, none at all (OK) Jackie. Hang on. Let me have a look.

Jackie: All right. Shall I keep count or shall you?

Lesley: No, you keep count. Ah (All right) now, there's something different with the window. The top window's only got one line across it and the bottom window's got two lines across it.

Jackie: OK, that's one. (Right. That's one) the window on the little house (Oh yes) next to it is missing...

Lesley: That's it. That's two.

Jackie: in the bottom picture. That's two.

Lesley: Oh lovely. Now, what about the scooter?

Jackie: The gate...the gate-post...

Lesley: What's different? Oh yes!

Jackie: Well...in the top one the top of the gate-post is white and in the bottom (And in the bottom it's black) it's black. That's three.,

Lesley: Great! (Erm) How about the scooter? Erm...the wheels are OK.

Jackie: The...the tr...if you look at the tree... (Mm) the top one's got one less leaf than the bottom one.

Lesley: Oh, you're right. Gosh, you are good at this (Yes) aren't you? (Mm. I agree) That's four. (That's four) Right. How about the...

Jackie: What about the road? (Yes) The... no, the line...

Lesley: Oh yes! On the left of the tree in the top one, there are two lines (Yes) to show the road and in the bottom there's only one. (The bottom one there's only one) That's five. (You've got one) Right. There's a dark line on the tree trunk (Uh-huh) in the bottom one and there isn't on the top one. (That's six) There's a dark line on the grass on the bottom one (Oh yes) but not on the top one.

Jackie: Just in front of the tree there.

Lesley: That's it. That's seven. (Seven) How many are there? (Ten) Ten! Oh gosh!

Jackie: The...there's a bit more on the road. In the top picture (Oh yes) there's a line in the bottom right-hand corner (Yes, but not in the bottom one) and it's missing in the bottom one. That's eight. (Eight)

Lesley: Now, the people...gosh! I can't see any differences with them at all.

Jackie: Uh, another two.

Lesley: Ah, yes, now. The girl in black has got... (A wh) a white collar in the top one and a black one in the bottom one. (Ah) Is that right? (That's good) That's nine. (Number nine) One more...oh! I can't find it.

Jackie: Nine...unless... (Are there any more) where is it? (There must be one more) Erm...we've got the one on the tree...

Lesley: Can't see anything different...

Jackie: Well, I suggest we erm...

Lesley: Well, let's give it up, or perhaps we could look in the back of the book.

Length: 2 min. 48 sec.
Number of speakers: 2.
Setting: Two friends doing puzzles.

Key language

Function: Describing people and locating things.

Lexis:
have fun	be missing
puzzle	gate-post
face	collar
top	give up
bottom	keep count
line	

Structures: he's...someone...
I thought of...
it's someone from...
the one at the bottom
the top...'s only got...
the bottom...'s got...
across...
next to...
if you look at the...

on the left of...
just in front of...
in the bottom right-hand corner
in the...one
the one on the...

TEACHING HINTS

Teach any items above that need revising or presenting by inventing or finding puzzles/pictures of your own similar to those in the Student's Book. If you can find two copies of a simple picture, you can draw in the differences yourself. Find a picture of a famous person in a magazine.

Tasks

Before listening

Ask students if they enjoy doing puzzles and if they are good at it. Tell students they are going to hear two friends doing puzzles together and tell them to open their books at page 50. Get them to guess the place (a bridge on the Thames in London) and the object (a pair of sunglasses) without the tape.

Listening task

Tell students to listen for the answers to the other puzzles. Tell them to write the name of the famous person and put a ring round each difference in the bottom picture. The final difference is not on tape, so encourage students to find it on their own. Let them check their answers with each other then with you.

Reading and writing tasks

Ask students if they like word games and puzzles and then to look at page 51 in their books. Tell them to work out the puzzles. When everyone has finished, ask them to read their answers aloud. Check that everyone has the same answers.

Listening

First of all try to guess the place and the object. These are not mentioned on the tape. Then identify the face.

Familiar Place... but where?

London

Familiar Face ... but whose?

King Hussein

Familiar Object... but what?

Sunglasses

They look the same but . . .

. . . there are ten differences between these two pictures. Can you spot them?

In the bottom picture put a ring around each difference mentioned. Try to find the missing difference not mentioned on the tape.

129

Reading and writing

Do these puzzles.

Jim's Christmas List

'What do you want for Christmas?' asked Jim's mother.

'Oh, all sorts of things,' replied Jim. 'I'll make a list of them.'

This he did, but his baby brother found the list and tore it into three strips, then tore the middle strip into eight pieces. His mother put the two large strips together, but they didn't make much sense.

Can *you* work out what Jim wanted for Christmas?

A Party Invitation

Can you read it?

Jim wants for Christmas:

1. cricket bat
2. bicycle lamp
3. fountain pen
4. box of sweets
5. ghost stories
6. poster paints
7. bow and arrows
8. motor boat

The invitation says:

Dear Pip,

We are having some friends to tea on Boxing Day and we hope you can come. I expect we shall play one or two jolly games and eat a great big cake which my mother is making. I will be overjoyed if you say yes.

Yours,
Laurie

Objectives

1 To help students to understand and follow descriptions of people and to identify the people concerned.
2 To give students practice in reading and completing a questionnaire about interests and preferences.

Tape

Tapescript

Policeman: Erm...you left an informal report with Sergeant Dawkins there's just a couple of things I'd like to check on. Erm... could you describe the girl to me in a bit more detail, please?

Witness: Er ... yes she was erm... darkish... erm... I should think she was between twenty-five and thirty (Mm) roundabout. And ... erm... she had shortish hair ... er ... I think she had a fringe ... bit untidy.

Policeman: Did you notice the clothing at all?

Witness: Er ... she had a white collar ...erm... open-necked shirt I think ... erm... or blouse and ...er... what looked like ...er... a velvet jacket but I can't remember the colour (I see) ...erm... I think it was a green or a brown but it was some dark colour.

Policeman: OK well let's go on to the ...erm... man now that you saw ...erm... if you could just describe him to me because there wasn't much on the report that you left with the sergeant.

Witness: Yes...erm... well he was ... I noticed he was wearing a funny kind of woollen jacket... (Mm) ...erm...

Policeman: A bulky sort of jacket was it? Thick knit or ...?

Witness: ...er ... well yes. I ... not really very bulky. It looked as if it was knitted and it had a sort of woollen collar and I think ...erm... he was wearing an open-necked shirt too... (Yes) ... erm... he was ...erm... younger than her ...er... I think ... (Yes) ... erm... I think he was about ... well I ...I should think he was in his early twenties.

Policeman: And she looked older?

Witness: She looked a bit older, to me. (I see) Erm... he had his hair brushed back.

Policeman: Yes. Anything about the shirt that you noticed ... was it just a plain white shirt or was it...?

Witness: I think it was striped but I can't be perfectly sure, (Mm) but I do remember his hair was ...erm... sort of wavy and ... erm... brushed back and shortish.

Policeman: OK, well that's fine. Thanks very much. If you ...erm... leave your phone number with the desk sergeant maybe we'll contact you in the near future.

Length: 2 min. 3 sec.
Number of speakers: 2.
Setting: A policeman interviewing a witness at the police station.

Key language

Function: Describing people's appearances.

Lexis:

darkish	knitted
shortish	white
fringe	plain
collar	striped
open-necked shirt	untidy
blouse	brushed back
jacket	wavy
woollen	twenties

Structures: he was wearing...
he had ...
it looked as if it was...
it looked...
it looked like...

TEACHING HINTS

Use magazine pictures or ones you have drawn yourself to teach the above lexis. Select one of the above structures and give further practice of this vocabulary while presenting the structure.

You could give further practice to both structures and lexis by playing a guessing game. You begin by saying 'I saw a famous man yesterday. He was wearing...' The students try to guess who you are thinking of and you continue describing him until one of them guesses correctly. The student who named him correctly begins the game again.

Tasks

Before listening

Set the scene for the tape by telling the students there has been a robbery and that the police are interviewing a witness. (You will have to teach 'witness'.) Elicit from students the type of questions the policeman would ask and write headings on the board, e.g. hair, face, clothing. This will revise the vocabulary taught at the beginning of this unit. Ask students to open their books at page 52. Encourage students to guess the jobs, ages, interests of the people in the pictures.

Listening task

Tell students to keep looking at the photographs while the tape is being played and to try to identify the two people described. Play the tape again and ask them to make lists of the key words they pick out, one list for the man and one for the woman. Check these lists and then draw students' attention to the details on the tape that they missed.

Reading task

Ask students to look at page 53. Tell them to read it through and underline any vocabulary they are not sure of. Then in pairs or groups ask them to clarify this vocabulary using a dictionary. Check with the whole class that there are no outstanding problems before moving on to the writing.

Writing task

Ask students to begin by answering question 1. Let them compare their answer with a partner. Tell them to go on to number 2 and to answer for themselves and for their partners. Let them compare answers. They can then move on to number 3. If there is time you may want to collate their answers and draw up a class profile of students' favourite activities and interests. Numbers 4 and 5 can either be done in class or at home. Prepare them by clarifying the instructions.

Listening

Tick the photographs of the man and woman described. Make two lists of the words that helped you make your choice, one list for the man and one for the woman.

┌─ *Man* ─────────────────
│
│ woollen jacket
│ open-necked shirt
│ striped shirt
│ early twenties
│ short wavy hair
│
└─────────────────────────

┌─ *Woman* ───────────────
│
│ 25–30
│ fringe
│ darkish/shortish hair
│ white collar
│ open-necked shirt
│ dark jacket
│
└─────────────────────────

Reading and writing

Fill in the questionnaire.
Compare answers with a neighbour.

Somewhere there is Someone who is Right for You.

DON'T GAMBLE ON FINDING YOUR IDEAL PARTNER

Start here

1 BY TICKING THE PHOTO THAT APPEALS MOST TO YOU

2 Do you consider yourself:

	Friend	You			
Shy.	☐	☐	Generous:	☐	☑
Extrovert:	☐	☑	Outdoor type:	☐	☑
Adventurous:	☐	☑	Creative:	☐	☑
Family type:	☑	☐	Practical:	☑	☐
Clothes-conscious:	☐	☐	Intellectual:	☑	☐

3 Indicate which activities and interests you enjoy by placing a '1' (one) in the appropriate box. If you dislike a particular activity, write a '0' (nought) in the box. If you have no preference, leave the column blank.

Pop music:	☐	Cinema:	1	Creative writing/ painting.	☐
Fashion:	1	Good food:	☐	Poetry.	☐
Pubs and clubs:	1	Politics:	☐	Philosophy/ Psychology/ Sociology	1
Sport.	1	Classical music:	1		
Pets:	0	Art/Literature:	1		
Folk music	☐	'Live' theatre:	☐	History/ Archeology:	☐
Jazz:	1	Science or technology:	☐	Conversation	☐
Travelling:	1				

4 BLOCK CAPITALS ONLY—ONE LETTER PER SPACE —LEAVE BLANKS WHEN REQUIRED

Your Sex **F** M or F
Your Age **19** yrs
Your Height **1** m **73** cm

Age I would like to meet **20** MIN **30** MAX

Christian Name (one only) **RUTH**
Surname **PARKER**
Address **3 JAMES STREET**
BASINGSTOKE
HANTS

Nationality **BRITISH** Religion **C of E**
Occupation **MUSIC STUDENT**

5 I enclose 2 first class stamps for postage of my free computer test and brochure. I am genuinely interested in finding my ideal partner.

SIGNED *R. Palmer*

Send today to: Dateline, Dept. (OBJ), Singles House, 23/25 Abingdon Rd., London, W.8. (01-937 6503)

LONDON PARIS BONN GENOA

Dateline leaves nothing to chance

135